MORAL ASPECTS
OF ECONOMIC GROWTH,
AND OTHER ESSAYS

THE WILDER HOUSE SERIES
IN POLITICS, HISTORY,
AND CULTURE

A volume in the Series

edited by David Laitin
George Steinmetz

A full list of titles in the series appears at the end of the book.

MORAL ASPECTS
OF ECONOMIC
GROWTH, AND
OTHER ESSAYS

BARRINGTON MOORE, JR.

Cornell University Press

Ithaca and London

*Open access edition funded by the National Endowment for the Humanities/
Andrew W. Mellon Foundation Humanities Open Book Program.*

First published 1998 by Cornell University Press

Library of Congress Cataloging-in-Publication Data
Moore, Barrington, 1913–
    Moral aspects of economic growth, and other essays / Barrington Moore, Jr.
    p. cm. — (The Wilder House series in politics, history, and culture)
    Includes index.
    ISBN-13: 978-0-8014-3376-4 (cloth) — ISBN-13: 978-1-5017-2641-5 (pbk.)
    1. Business ethics—England—History. 2. Social ethics. I. Title. II. Series.
HF5387.M637   1998
174'.4'0941—dc21   97-45210

To the memory of E.C.M. 1913–1992

Contents

Preface

All of these essays have to do with issues of authority, inequality, and justice, issues that have preoccupied me since my days as a graduate student at Yale University before the Second World War. All along I have made a strong effort to eschew lamentations in favor of explanations, though I do believe that a true explanation can make somebody lament. The opening essay, "Moral Aspects of Economic Growth," represents the beginning of a large-scale comparative historical study that I had to abandon. The others are, I hope, reasonably self-contained and comprehensible as such. "Austerity and Unintended Riches" appeared in *Comparative Studies in Society and History* 29, no. 4 (October 1987), 787–810; none of the other essays has been published before, though two have been given as public lectures. With one exception, "Bequests of the Twentieth Century to the Twenty-first," which was written around the end of 1996, all the essays (including the two lectures) were written before 1992. The reader can judge how well, if at all, they have weathered the intervening years.

On the night after Valentine's Day 1992 Elizabeth Carol Moore died. She had been "home editor" and much more to me for almost fifty years. This book carries no acknowledgments except to her.

BARRINGTON MOORE, JR.

Cambridge, Massachusetts

MORAL ASPECTS
OF ECONOMIC GROWTH,
AND OTHER ESSAYS

Moral Aspects of Economic Growth: Historical Notes on Business Morality in England

This essay seeks to describe and account for the moral codes and patterns of behavior among the leaders in English commerce and industry during two widely separated periods of history. Though the emphasis is on the period of the industrial revolution (roughly from 1760 to 1860), in order to understand what was distinctive about that crucial epoch it is necessary to know the central features of commercial organization and practice in the preindustrial world. Hence the essay begins with some glances at the moral problems of medieval business from the early fourteenth to the seventeenth centuries.

I chose the medieval period partly because it was remote enough in time from the industrial revolution and could thus be expected to display some revealing contrasts and continuities. Another reason was the quality of the sources. The Selden Society has published a large quantity of primary source materials in the form of laws to control trade.[1] They shed much light on the moral problems faced by men in trade during these early centuries. There is also a splendid monograph by Sylvia L. Thrupp, *The Merchant Class of Medieval London [1300–1500]*, which provides detailed information on the economic, political, and social life of the merchants, their moral codes, and their actual behavior.[2]

Any moral code provides a description, justification, and explanation

---

[1]See Charles Gross, ed., *Select Cases Concerning the Law Merchant, 1251–1779*, 3 vols. (London, 1908–1932). John Selden (1584–1654) was a distinguished legal scholar and antiquarian who supported the House of Commons during the Civil War but earned the respect of both sides. Throughout this essay citations to often-referenced works will in many cases be given parenthetically in the text, though the first full citation will reside in a footnote.

[2]Ann Arbor, Mich., 1948; paperback, 1962.

of how human society ought to work. Ordinarily a moral code by itself has little to say directly about how the society it purports to guide and instruct actually does work. Yet to the extent that it contains a description of evil behavior and its supposed causes, the code will shed valuable light on the actual behavior in that society.

The most important function of any moral code is to condemn and, if possible, prohibit certain specified forms of behavior. Such behavior may seem to be effective in the short run by yielding quick results, as in the case of a successful theft, or it may yield at least short-term pleasure, as in the case of an adulterous affair. From this standpoint violations of the moral code may seem to the individual to be shortcuts to desirable ends, but according to the moral code such shortcuts are judged to be harmful to the social order as a whole. In many human societies, though not in all, theft and adultery (the latter often considered a form of theft) are perceived and punished as anti-social acts.

The specification of certain kinds of behavior as anti-social has usually had a religious component and often a religious sanction. Ordinary people do not as a rule say that theft is evil because it is anti-social. They say that God or the gods forbid theft (usually a quite specific form of theft, such as stealing a horse) and will punish the thief in this life or the life to come or both.

The type of society one ought to strive for is defined to a great extent by the moral code adopted by the members of the society. This code also specifies the types of people and kinds of behavior the members of this society are expected either to love or to hate. In this way it defines the presumed threats to the social order.

In the record of human history, especially if we include the anthropological record, there can appear to be a bewildering variety of moral codes. It may be useful to outline briefly the huge historical transformation that forms the context of the moral changes and continuities to be discussed in this essay.

For centuries Europe had been under the rule of soldiers, with considerable assistance from the priesthood. The moral code of premodern Europe (and of many other parts of the world) was a military aristocratic one with strong religious overtones. Those who fought, or more accurately those who controlled the fighters, exercised what social control existed, which was very little indeed, until kings or rulers began to strengthen their power. Those who fought dealt with, and at times created, the main problems threatening this world. It was the task of the priesthood to take care of those in the next world. By various means the governing classes extracted a surplus of food and other products from the main economic producers: peasants and, somewhat later, artisans.

Under this system, and indeed in all premodern social systems, there was not much anyone could do to increase production and thereby raise the level of consumption. Cultivating land that had been left fallow was important but hardly led to changes comparable to those of the industrial revolution. Instead the main way for those with political clout to increase their share of the valuable goods of this world was through armed theft. One conquered some new territory and extracted tribute from it. This was essentially a zero-sum situation. Whatever the conqueror gained the conquered lost.

Thus in preindustrial societies the main ways to gain wealth were to take it away from someone else or to force someone else—slaves, serfs, or other forms of controlled labor—to create wealth and turn it over to their masters. Even the Age of Discoveries, with its heavy emphasis on discovering new wealth, did not, so far as I can make out, produce any alternative to this rule of steal, oppress, or go without. Only with the industrial revolution did some men come to realize that it was possible to create wealth and new forms of wealth, such as machinery and coal mines, through their own collective efforts. The new way of creating wealth seemed less glamorous than the dashing military-aristocratic device of armed theft. Also a good many workers in the new mines and factories felt that budding industrial society merely introduced a new form of oppression barely masked by the wage contract. Hence, the coming of industrialism did not bring about universal rejoicing. Capitalists had a hard time promoting their virtues and those of the new era against the suspicions of both the older landed elites and many of their own workers.

Contrary to the hopes of some nineteenth-and even twentieth-century optimists, creating new wealth has by no means driven armed theft out of existence. Instead in the course of the twentieth century, the aristocratic element just about disappeared as armed theft became democratic and plebeian, especially in fascist movements and fascist regimes, though not only in these.

During the eighteenth and nineteenth centuries representatives of the older military, aristocratic ethic at times treated the new leaders in commerce and business with condescension and contempt. Spokesmen for the new business leaders responded with claims to the effect that their way of life would end the days of the military-aristocratic ethic and usher in an age of peace among nations. Snobbish contempt and utopian dreams were not, as we shall see, the only responses to this historical transformation in the means and forms of production. For the moment the most important point to make is this: by the time that the industrial revolution had acquired enough momentum to appear irreversible, say about 1850, or after the "hungry forties," it had increased the supply of goods and services to the point where, at least in England, disputes over their distribution had ceased to be a major threat to social stability. Before this time no social ethic had grown up against such a background of peace and at least potential plenty. Respectability was about to triumph. Our story will come to an end just as the triumph has begun to seem obvious.[3]

The Medieval Background

To begin our historical survey of the actual practices of British business morality in the late Middle Ages let us cast a critical glance at some of the legal cases collected by the Selden Society. Here and elsewhere in this essay I emphasize forms of behavior that contemporaries defined as illegal and immoral, because what a code forbids is generally its most revealing feature. Prohibitions tell us what is expected to cause trouble at a specific time and in a specific place.

In England during the Middle Ages the courts most concerned with commercial activities were known as "piepowder" courts, although by the mid-thirteenth century "statutes merchant" to some degree preempted them. "Piepowder" comes from the French *pieds poudrés* and refers to the dusty feet of wandering merchants, who were hardly more than peddlers in the early days. In England these courts were set up by the king. Their jurisdiction included actions concerning debt, contract, trespass, and breaches of the assize of bread and beer.[4] An assize was a statute regulating the weight, measure, ingredients, and price of articles sold in the market. Thus an assize was a crucial element in the widespread medieval attempt to control economic activity in accord with ethical standards. The frequency of violations indicates that the ethical effort was not too successful.

The piepowder courts were courts for merchants, and they were run by merchants, that is, men familiar with the ways of business. Hence these courts were able to render speedy justice, a big advantage in a situation where merchants were highly mobile. It was not unusual for a merchant

[3]See the excellent account by F. M. L. Thompson, *The Rise of Respectable Society: A Social History of Victorian Britain, 1830–1900* (Cambridge, Mass., 1988).
[4]Gross, *Select Cases*, 1:xxiii–xxiv.

to run up a sizable debt and then abscond. To use a modern vernacular, there were plenty of deadbeats around. That was one good reason for speedy justice, as well as for a system largely administered by the merchants themselves. As early as the twelfth century in some parts of England and Scotland, custom required that pleas concerning wayfaring merchants be settled before the third tide.[5]

Merchants evidently regarded royal courts, which were not limited to piepowder courts, as a great improvement over the wager of law. As the traditional way of establishing the "truth" in medieval judicial disputes over large parts of Europe, the wager of law deserves a brief description to show what the merchants were opposing. The essence of the procedure was this: the defendant, when denying an accusation under oath, appeared before the court surrounded by a number of companions, called *jurators*, *compurgators*, and other names, who swore, not as persons who knew the facts—knowledge they often lacked completely—"but as sharers and partakers in the oath of denial." Thus we learn that in 899 a German queen Uta "cleared herself of an accusation of infidelity by taking a purgatorial oath with eighty-two nobles."[6]

Though the wager of law was obviously a very cumbersome and uncertain way of settling mercantile issues such as uncollected debts, in England a guild might be dragged into a wager of law since guild members sometimes felt that an accusation of this type against one member was an attack on the entire membership. Therefore members had to serve as compurgators (Lea, 39–40).

On the other hand, the numerous cases adduced by Lea overwhelmingly concern individuals from the higher reaches of premercantile society: the monarchy, the nobility, and the clergy. Under Anglo-Saxon jurisprudence "the number and quality of the conjugators were regulated according to the nature of the crime and the rank of the accused." The value of a man's oath depended on his rank, "that of a thane, for instance, being equal to those of seven yeoman" (Lea, 43–44). The guiding principle that trustworthiness depended on social rank seems at times to have had an odd twist inasmuch as it required more compurgators to clear a monarch or queen (as noted above) of a serious accusation than was necessary for an ordinary nobleman.

---

[5]Gross, *Select Cases*, I:xxv; see also xxvi. For a specific case in 1458 see 122–126. For a full picture of general procedures and issues before such courts see xxviii–xxxiii.

[6]Henry C. Lea, *Superstition and Force: Essays on The Wager of Law; The Wager of Battle; The Ordeal; Torture* (3d edition, Philadelphia, 1878), 31–32, 35, 37–38.

To the ordinary merchant this grading of justice by rank would have been hateful and inconvenient. If someone owed the merchant 500 pounds sterling, the merchant did not care about the man's status. He wanted his 500 pounds without giving the debtor time to hunt up a set of compurgators. If astute he knew that a debtor of high status had numerous ways to avoid paying debts. A less discerning merchant could ruin himself.

The wager of law as a whole appears to have been an expedient resorted to in cases where it was hard to decide who was right and who was wrong. There are some indications that the wager of law may have disappeared over time by turning compurgators into a jury of twelve peers or social equals. While it had ceased to be important as early as the close of the twelfth century, it was not formally abrogated until 1833 (Lea, 49, 64, 80).

Returning now to mercantile morality we find that in England during the Middle Ages failure to pay debts was regarded as an immoral act, punished publicly. Every fair or market was required to have a pillory and a tumbril for punishing debtors. In its older meaning tumbril was a type of chair used for punishing dishonest tradesmen (and others) by fastening them in it to be pelted. The purpose was not merely to take vengeance and inflict pain on shady characters; there was a heavy emphasis on making a public spectacle and negative example out of them, thereby reaffirming the socially approved economic virtue of honesty and exposing moral defects to public censure (Gross, 1:xxiv).

A moral distinction between the provident and improvident debtor appears in the judicial correspondence and records of the fourteenth and fifteenth centuries (Gross, 3:xxviii). The debtor's prison was a recognized instrument against political offenders as well at this time. Yet it was hard to arrest irresponsible debtors. Kindred and/or competing creditors could find many ways of hiding such offenders or of helping them to flee (Gross, 3:xxxi).

If even an irresponsible debtor could count on this degree of social support, the moral and legal rules about paying debts could hardly have commanded unanimous agreement. The rules themselves provided several loopholes. Responsible debtors might be placed under loose arrest in their own or their creditor's house. There was a statutory obligation on the creditor to feed the debtor for three months. There is said to be no evidence from medieval times of the tragedy of an improvident debtor's hopeless captivity (Gross, 3:xxxi).

Though the evidence is late, it is worth noticing that crooked lenders existed alongside debtors who failed to pay up. The crooked lender found his opportunities because debtors were often careless about obtaining a receipt for the payment of a debt. This carelessness enabled an unscrupulous creditor to present the same charge over and over again and even enforce payment for want of a receipt. In an effort to put a stop to this practice under James I (reigned 1603–1625) traders were compelled to cancel in their ledgers debts that had been paid (Gross, 3:xxx-xxxi).

As might be expected, there were also numerous complaints about the merchants' fraudulent manipulation of weights and measures. For example, they might buy by using a large weight and sell by a small one. Charges of fraud were not limited to merchants; bailiffs of manors also faced such charges. Such complaints seem to have been most serious and persistent from the middle of the fourteenth to the middle of the fifteenth centuries (Gross, 2:xlv–xlvii).

Though the Middle Ages saw the establishment of special courts and special legislation for merchants, business morality remained rooted in a larger system of morality and was heavily influenced by some of its leading ideas. One of these was the notion of personal honor and its opposite — shame. A series of cases ranging in time from an Elizabethan Plea Roll back to a thirteenth-century fair court shows that a plaintiff "would not have the shame put upon him" (Gross, 2: xli). Damage to reputation was just as important as material damage. Under capitalism the businessman also felt great concern for his reputation. This concern forms a striking example of moral continuity between the medieval and modern eras.

The sovereign was expected to show traditional solicitude not only for the material but also for the moral welfare of his or her subjects. National repute and well-being, like that of the individual, depended on personal honor and integrity. But this social reputation was constantly endangered by the greed and cunning of a few, which led to the general corruption of many, despite the paternal warnings of the Church and the fraternal efforts of the guilds. The edicts of the king in Parliament and the severe sentences of his justices in court, bench, or eyre (circuit court) failed to cure and even aggravated the evil.

As the summary of contemporary opinion shows, the Church was the source of traditional morality governing business affairs, while secular and royal courts provided the main sanctions. Another source of moral rules, not mentioned in this capsule account of public opinion but obvious from the rest of the legal materials discussed so far, arose from the day-to-day transactions among the merchants themselves. The granting of credit and collection of debts created definitions of prudent and imprudent, acceptable and unacceptable ways of conducting business.

We may conclude these observations on the business morality of pre-industrial merchants, as refracted through the laws, with a sketch of the history of legal attitudes toward the purchase of stolen goods. This evidence shows clearly the influence of mercantile needs and moral judgments on the law. Neither Roman nor Germanic law protected the merchant who had in good faith bought stolen goods against the claims of the original owner. In England, as late as the thirteenth century, stolen goods could be recovered, not only from the original thief but from the hands of the third, fourth, and twentieth possessor, even though these hands were clean and the purchase had taken place in the open market. The law indicates that theft and fraud were major concerns in medieval England. Obviously such a law hampered both sale and barter. As one historian has observed, "Commercial business cannot be carried on if we have to inquire into the title of everybody who comes to us with documents of title, such as bills of lading or for the sale of goods."[7]

In addition to the merchants' own efforts, two factors helped to change this situation. One was the influence of the Church, which stressed the importance of good faith in these and other business transactions. The other was the financial interests or necessities of the feudal lords of the market. Fairs and markets were valuable sources of revenue to the feudal lord. Protecting the honest purchaser in the possession of his goods was likely to attract merchants, increase the importance of his fair and hence its revenue. By 1291 it appears that the principle of bona fide possession had become part of England's law merchant though not yet of its common law. The protection extended to sales in market and fair, and was at first limited to them. Later it was extended in many towns on the continent to all places (including shops) where commercial transactions took place. In England it eventually became a privilege recognized by the common law.[8]

* * * * *

Up to this point in our exposition the available information concerns mainly a population of traveling merchants. They move with their goods from one place to another, trying to buy cheap and sell dear. By and large they do not make anything but distribute for a profit what others have made. The earliest merchants were probably travelers, as suggested by the reference to "dusty feet" in the term "piepowder." The unavailability lo-

---

[7]W. Mitchell, *An Essay on the Early History of the Law Merchant* (Cambridge, U.K. 1904), 93, 97, quoting Scrutton, *Mercantile Law*, 23.

[8]Mitchell, *Essay on Early History*, 97, 99–101.

cally of many sorts of goods because of primitive systems of transport could have provided an impetus to these merchant activities.

With the widespread rise in productivity that put in an appearance in the eleventh century more and more goods were produced in urban and proto-urban centers for local and regional consumption. A few of these urban growing points became not only centers of production but also centers of distribution, especially for imported goods. When such cities also housed the monarch and the monarch's central administrative staff, judicial authorities, and, in some cases, budding legislative organs, such a city became a metropolis by prevailing standards.[9] London was one of these. It was thickly settled, in both senses of the word. For the most part its inhabitants lived cheek by jowl alongside one another. And for the most part they also stayed put, though there were some drifters at the bottom of the economic scale and perhaps a few world-travelers on political and economic errands for those at the very top. At any rate during the Middle Ages a thin crust of well-to-do merchants, perhaps a little over six thousand, including their wives, children, and apprentices, dominated an urban population made up of other citizens in company livery with their wives, children, and apprentices, totaling perhaps seven thousand persons and small masters with their miscellaneous dependents, estimated at nearly twenty thousand persons.[10] The main line of fracture and conflict in this social setting fell between the merchant elite and the much larger number of small masters with their dependents. Corresponding to this fracture the main concern of the merchant elite was the maintenance of law and order. Law and order appears to have been what morality was all about (Thrupp, 75, 77).

Against this general background we shall in the rest of this essay analyze first the individual ethic of members of the merchant elite and then their collective ethic or sense of responsibility toward the society as a whole. So far as the evidence permits, we shall try to understand their actual behavior, with emphasis on the extent to which it departed from prevailing ethnic norms. Although analytically distinguishable, individual and collective ethics were closely connected.

As a town developed industries dependent on distant markets for their

[9]According to the *Oxford Universal Dictionary* (3d ed., 1955) the term "metropolis" first came into use in the 15th century, referring to the see of a metropolitan bishop. The first use of "metropolis," according to *Webster's Ninth New Collegiate Dictionary* (Springfield, Mass., 1983) occurred in the fourteenth century and "metropolitan" in the sense of a bishop or his see in the fifteenth century.

[10]Figures from Thrupp, *Merchant Class*, 51.

supplies or the sale of their products, the merchants scrambled to the top of the social heap and gained an important role in running the government of the city. These merchants had a "sufficiency," that is, enough wealth to contribute to public charges. The more sufficient and able were simultaneously seen as the better people, or morally superior. The moral epithet was specifically political and added a flavor of respectability.[11] "The better people," as Thrupp puts it, "were the more honest, the wiser, the more prudent, and the more discreet." This was no mere empty and traditional formula. Before any man could attain the legal status of an enfranchised citizen—generally a very small minority among the inhabitants of medieval cities—he had to show proof of at least some positive qualification on each of these scores. (pp. 14–15). In other words, he had to demonstrate moral, political, and economic qualifications. The economic ones were indispensable. By themselves, on the other hand, they did not guarantee the existence of the moral and political ones that were equally necessary for membership in the merchant elite.

These qualities were also the bases of legitimate authority and social inequality in the urban scene. Both religious teaching and the experience of apprenticeship stressed submission to authority, evidently regarded as a major virtue in the somewhat turbulent society of medieval London. Good behavior meant holding one's temper, especially before inferiors or superiors. The merchant, as we saw, liked to think of himself as prudent and discreet, rather like many a relatively undistinguished present-day banker. And the prudent man was always careful about the opinion of others (Thrupp, 164–165). In practice, attitudes toward authority varied from subservient to resentful. In all forms they were extraordinarily emotional, a description that suggests Florence more than London. The obligation to obey, Thrupp suggests, was not regarded as a rational matter. Instead it was a deep-grounded but purely personal matter. Perhaps because the level of resentment was high and obedience problematical, disobedience or disrespect to any figure of authority—parent, lord, master, magistrate—was held to be a sin (Thrupp, 16).

Day-to-day business ethics of course emphasized the prudent use of money. (If the imprudent use makes someone very rich, that is less serious, as long as there is no sign of dishonesty.) The medieval merchant

[11]This flavor of respectability has persisted as a desired attribute among leaders in business ever since the Middle Ages. A respectable person is creditworthy. He steers clear of socially visible sexual liaisons that distract attention from business. Only the flamboyantly successful can afford to flout the rules of respectability. This anti-erotic strain may have Christian origins, which in the beginning had nothing to do with business.

class did not, on the other hand, generate any gospel of hard work. Nor was there any puritanical ban on amusement as such. There was, however, some concern lest young men pick up habits of dissipation, and commercialized amusements, such as bear-baiting, cock-fighting, and wrestling. Gambling, including betting on the outcome of these amusements, was regarded as especially dangerous. Apprentices were forbidden to play with cards or dice. Discipline over apprentices also prohibited sexual liaisons (Thrupp, 174, 166–167, 169). Thus, like the expectations of virtue, the temptations to sin were stratified according to class membership.

Economic activities included a variety of sins. Contemporary preachers reproved the giving of short measure, misrepresentation, trading on holidays, and the practice of usury (Thrupp, 174–175). These practices linked ordinary and probably universal forms of dishonesty with historically specific prohibitions such as usury. Since Thrupp does not mention any sign of popular or religious hostility to merchants as people who create nothing while buying cheap and selling dear, it seems likely that medieval Londoners had outgrown that particular prejudice which had made sinners of all merchants. In any case many London merchants were producers in the sense of directing several forms of artisanal production, such as that by bakers, brewers, carpenters, saddlers, and many others. (For a longer list see Thrupp, 46.) There was in fact no aristocratic prejudice among merchants in medieval England against making money by working, although among the gentry some prejudice did exist. Among town and country gentlemen, there was strong prejudice against men engaged in retail trade (Thrupp, 243–244, 263–264).

Thus the English merchant elite did not have to struggle hard to establish the acceptability of a business morality over against an aristocratic, agrarian, and military ethic. Relations with the Church and religious morality were not quite so easy, as shown by religious hostility to usury. Yet there was not much of an attempt to enforce rules against usury, partly because it was hard to decide what usury really was. As for other business practices, the religious authorities advocated ordinary honesty plus charity toward the poor, attitudes widely acceptable to the merchants anyway. Merchants wanted the prayers of as many poor people as possible. They also felt that the poor were somehow blessed, a sentiment that disappeared with the advent of machine driven factories (Thrupp, 79, 175–177, 179).

As Thrupp points out, the merchants' attitude toward the poor was curiously mixed. Their sense that the poor were somehow blessed *and* capable of violent upheaval suggests that the merchants were somewhat uncertain about their own social status and the justifications for it. As we shall see in due course, some factory owners of the early nineteenth century seem to have gained confidence in their social worth by shedding traditional obligations to the social order.

In medieval London, economic status was in large measure moral status, especially in the higher reaches of the social hierarchy, and also quite obviously toward the bottom of the hierarchy. There were unsavory occupations, contact with which could disqualify a youngster for apprenticeship. Mercers banned country peddlers because they were suspected of handling stolen goods. Vagrant beggars were equally suspect. Mercers, who appear to have been especially touchy on these matters and especially afraid of pollution, also counted unfree birth, lameness, leprosy, and loss of an eye as defects that disqualified a lad for membership in their company (Thrupp, 217).

It would be a mistake to think that the sons of the merchant elite stepped easily onto the upper rungs of the social ladder. With little to inherit they often had to succeed on their own. Hence restlessness and driving ambition became prominent character traits among these men. They were traits that aroused widespread antagonism among spokesmen for the traditional precommercial society. Moralists felt it their duty to check the resulting individualistic and family ambitions. The chivalric literature of the time presented a negative image of the merchant, stressing avarice, ambition, and narrow absorption in the pursuit of money and power (Thrupp, 312–317, esp. 315). Evidently some familiar criticisms of "modern" society are centuries old.

In these criticisms of a socially corrosive individualism we encounter, perhaps for the first time, the conflict between a traditional ethic, whose standard is some form of public virtue or the public good, and an emergent modern ethic, whose standard is the individual's or family's attainments by its own efforts. In the course of economic growth the emphasis on the family would recede in favor of pure individualism. The conception of the social good and social obligations would also undergo marked transformation. By the twentieth century the main conceptions of the social good took the forms of liberalism (with a new emphasis on social responsibility for the unfortunate), fascism, or communism. Through these permutations, however, the conflict between social obligations and individual ambitions has remained an underlying theme.

This extended survey of the merchant's individual ethic reveals a set of demands and prohibitions expected (or hoped) to produce a character suitable for a specific social order. In addition to these character-shaping requirements, whose effectiveness is not always clear and was certainly less than total, London's medieval merchants faced a series of quite specific social obligations. On paper at least, they had to do certain things for the common good, no matter what the personal inclinations of these men were.

The city authorities, strongly influenced by the merchant elite, exercised jurisdiction over trade and industry. This collective authority had four aims. The first was to ensure an adequate food supply at reasonable prices by supervision of the market. The second was to enforce standards in manufacturing to protect the interests of consumers. The third was to prevent monopoly among the merchants and collective bargaining among the workers. The fourth and last aim was the control of brokerage rates (Thrupp, 92–93).

These regulations were a series of attempts to control the process of production and sale, that is, the behavior of the merchants for the benefit of the consumers. They had a clear ethical and political grounding: to keep prices down and maintain quality at levels sufficient to prevent popular discontent from exploding into dangerous riots. The policy of economic control for the sake of social peace—the working definition of the public good—was only a qualified success. There was a struggle between artisans and merchants that came to a head in 1376. With some minor concessions the merchants won hands down (Thrupp, 74–77, 80–81, 84).

Granting that the economic controls (along with other devices no doubt) did work well enough to prevent serious social disorder, what was their actual mode of operation? There was considerable difference from one kind of commodity to another. There is some reason to suspect that each trade had its own pattern of frauds, well known to well-placed insiders, while individuals with low status, such as most women, were unable to do anything about them (Thrupp, 173). Brewers were the target of continual complaints that they were selling ale above the official price. Meat was easier to supervise because its sale was concentrated in certain places. Bread prices were controlled by intermittent tests of the costs of baking it. But the tests were not or could not be done often enough to be effective. Instead the price of bread was allowed to fluctuate, subject only to the control of public opinion or, more accurately, public clamor.

According to Thrupp, the only price regulations that seriously affected merchant companies were those in the retail fish trade. These were politically important since, next to bread, fish was the most important food for the poor. But the mayor who interfered much with the fishmongers had to be a strong one. Fishmongers were proud of their own court and preferred to deal with offenders directly. They had their own complicated rules for the fair distribution of the catch and their own wardens sworn to search out violators. Nevertheless in the first half of the fourteenth century, groups of fishmongers were on several occasions "prosecuted before the mayor for selling outside prescribed market places and for using baskets of short measure." With the exception of the fishmongers, and in one instance, the grocers, none of the merchant companies were kept under the supervision of the mayor. While acknowledging the formal authority of the mayor and aldermen over all their activities, the merchant companies in practice were left to frame what by-laws they chose and allowed to enforce them in their own way (Thrupp, 95, 96).

The power of the merchants' fraternities was widely feared because it was known to be used for selfish purposes. Commercial fraud, forestalling of food supplies on the way to the market, slander, breach of an oath, and rudeness to magistrates were widespread offenses. Yet "money and position could nearly always protect an offender's personal dignity." By paying fines, bakers, for example, could escape the degrading penalty of being pilloried "for selling loaves of poor quality or short weight." In fact cases of commercial fraud among merchants rarely came before city courts because the merchants' own courts were supposed to deal with the problem and thereby avoid public scandal (Thrupp, 21, 24). Acting in accord with the wishes of the merchant elite and citizen masters, the city government made repeated attempts to suppress the competition of petty dealers who set up unauthorized street markets. The wealthy engaged in tax evasion on a substantial scale, thereby revealing that in practice there were definite limits to the public obligations of the prosperous (Thrupp, 72, 89).

As one looks back over these attempts to create and enforce a sense of economic obligation to the society as a whole, one can hardly avoid the conclusion that the effort was mainly a failure, mitigated here and there by sporadic attempts at enforcement. It was also a sham, though probably not a deliberate deception, insofar as a generally accepted ethic of fair prices and adherence to standards of quality made rule by the merchant elite generally acceptable. Meanwhile rule by the merchants made it easier for them to cheat without detection. To a degree then the ethic of honesty in business was self-defeating because it increased the institutional opportunities for evasion. Still this explanation in terms of ideas and ethical beliefs fails to reveal a crucial aspect of the story. Why was enforcement so erratic and feeble? It is not enough to reply that the merchant elite was the government and could not be expected to enforce measures counter to its own interests and inclinations, even though that is true. The city government at that time could not draw on enough other social forces to hold the merchants in check, because other organized social groupings scarcely existed. (The national government was not a great deal better off.) Only when the state has become strong enough to draw on other interest groups is there any hope of enforcing business morality in an effective and widespread manner. That situation has not yet become dominant in any major capitalist country, although there have been many changes for the better since the days of medieval London. Nevertheless where business remains the predominant activity in the modern state, we can expect businessmen as individuals to engage in a great deal of selfish, unethical, and asocial behavior.

Themes in Medieval Business

Three themes stand out in this review of the conduct of business in medieval England and the ethical notions about this conduct. The first concern of the merchant seems to have been to collect his debts. At least getting his hands on what another merchant owed him was a serious and continuing concern, a sticky point in the process of doing business. The moral obligation to pay one's debts seems to have been rather less than overwhelming.

In the second place, the ideal moral personality of the time strongly emphasized the virtues of prudence and obedience to authority. Though such writers could provide a congenial base for later Protestant and Puritan conceptions of work as a religious commandment or as yielding a precious sign of salvation, that special mingling of God and work still lay mainly over the historical horizon. Nor was the English medieval merchant an ascetic, fearfully avoiding the pleasures of the table, the bottle, and the bed. Furthermore there are no signs here of the swashbuckling economic buccaneer, the man who overrode all legal, moral, and social obstacles to create for himself an enormous fortune or an economic satrapy. If such individuals ever were important in English social history, which seems to me doubtful, they must have come to the surface later.

From the standpoint of our investigation, the third point is the most interesting. In theory, English medieval business morality emphasized strongly what today would be called the social responsibility of business. The idea found expression mainly in regulations governing the market, which attempted to assure the good quality of artisans' products and especially a sufficient supply of food at prices the poor could afford to pay. This medieval version of *Sozialpolitik* was an attempt to maintain social peace and order. More precisely it was an effort to ward off popular riots and upheavals in a society where the dominant strata lacked dependable means for repression.

The policy did not work. There was one major popular outbreak during the late fourteenth century, as Thrupp indicates (pp. 75–79). This outbreak did not work either, in the sense that it failed to bring about a redistribution of power and authority or a change in policy. Finally, the attempts to assure good quality and low prices (mainly for food) also did not work. Here the reason for failure or, at the very least, inefficiency is quite plain. The enforcement of measures affecting prices and quality was in the hands of the guilds that produced the goods. It was in the interest of the guilds to keep prices up and quality down insofar as they could do so without too severe a loss of reputation. There was no power outside the guilds strong enough to police their activities. If the city fathers tried to bring a major guild up short, there could have been an explosion. In any case the city fathers were unlikely to try any serious efforts at law enforcement on their own because they were either officers of important guilds themselves or were tied to guild leaders by friendship, kinship, or business connections. Hence the much praised "organic" and "cooperative" nature of medieval society, which supposedly contrasts so favorably with modern individualist and selfish capitalism, turns out to be a rather ramshackle fraud.

With these reservations we may leave the medieval scene and move toward that of the industrial revolution. The constraints of time and space allow no more than a fleeting glance at the most relevant developments of the period between the Middle Ages and the beginnings of the industrial revolution.

During the sixteenth and seventeenth centuries the power of the central government increased, though there was at least one temporary reverse during the Civil War (1642–1648), especially when the fighting was severe. Increased power made it possible for a government to extract heavier levies from its subject population. Indeed the government became by far the most effective agency for extracting and collecting a surplus (or the difference between what was produced and what was consumed) from the subordinate population. English royal absolutism did not develop as far along this path as its French counterpart. English royal absolutism was also relatively short-lived. Nevertheless it became the magnet for businessmen who wanted to get rich by getting a post in the royal apparatus to siphon off some of this surplus into their own pockets. As Francis Bacon put it, "The ways to enrich be many, and most of them foul."[12]

In this situation shady deals and morally ambiguous behavior flourished. To some extent the moral ambiguity may have been due to the fact that moral standards as we have come to know them had not yet been firmly established. The distinction between public resources and private property seems at times to have been rather faint. Or, to put the point more accurately, it was much easier for malcontents who were not profiting from the system to recognize and attack shady deals than it was for insiders to defend themselves while they were making a good thing out of their position. The malcontent's motives may not have been disinterested. Yet their moral indignation reveals the existence in some quarters of standards we can recognize.[13]

It is possible that the English state offered more temptation for corrupt practices than its French counterpart because the English king commanded fewer resources and lacked the bureaucratic means to oversee expenditures and policy that were available to the French monarchy. Tawney put his finger on the decisive features of the English situation in words that suggest this comparison. "It was the opportunities for speculation offered by the co-existence of an embarrassed Exchequer with a mass of valuable rights of which Governments could dispose, and an ambitious structure of economic regulation which they lacked the means to enforce that produced the unstable compound which provides the material for most of Cranfield's deals."[14] Meanwhile the Crown had drifted into a position of dependence on businessmen. James I had no affection for them, but he was well aware that without them he could not keep afloat. The Crown had "necessities to meet and favours to bestow." Favors were necessary to maintain the Crown's prestige and public support. They were also expensive. Then there were needs for increased revenue and loans to meet emergencies, as well as for expert advice on tariffs, currency, credit, commercial diplomacy, the prospects of the textile industries, and several other issues. All this money and advice could only come from capitalists at home in the intricacies of the ambiguous *demi-monde* between politics, business, and fashionable society.[15]

[12]Quoted by R. H. Tawney, *Business and Politics under James I: Lionel Cranfield as Merchant and Minister* (Cambridge University Press, 1958), 116.

[13]These points recur throughout Tawney, *Business and Politics*, esp. chap. 8 on Cranfield's impeachment and fall.

[14]Ibid., 85.

[15]Ibid., 80–81. Not mentioned here, fashionable society is discussed elsewhere in Tawney.

One could make a case for calling business under this system parasitic, because it did not increase the quantity of goods and services, not even by trade. (To be fair to Cranfield it is necessary to point out that he made substantial and effective efforts to make his segments of the bureaucracy more efficient.) Against the notion of parasitism one might point out that the great discoveries, mainly a feature of Elizabeth's reign, must have brought more wealth into the British body politic, a transfusion that picked up again in the eighteenth century. This observation may be quite correct, but it does not detract from the point toward which I am working. So far as I can see, this essentially parasitic symbiosis between business and the monarchy could have continued more or less indefinitely. Put bluntly, for the businessman to make money, the best strategy was to get a place at the political trough. This strategy has never completely disappeared. Probably it never will, but during the latter part of the eighteenth century it began to recede into the background. That happened because better ways of making money arose. Historians still refer to these better ways as the industrial revolution.

The Age of Tinkers and Inventors

Before looking at the concrete problems facing businessmen in the early years of industrialism I want to comment briefly on the sources. They are reasonably good. There are useful biographies of several major figures in the industrial revolution. Most valuable for a study of early capitalist ways of thinking are two sets of Parliamentary hearings, one on child labor in 1816 and another on more general economic issues in 1833. Finally there is a rich study of provincial capitalist mores, based in large measure on unpublished local materials.[16] All this material is welcome, rewarding, and, for the most part, interesting. Nevertheless it is surprising that we do not have a great deal more information. Actually there has been precious little research on the ways businessmen have carried out and thought about their work. That may be partly because businessmen have often been taciturn, platitudinous, or both. In comparison with even the silliest social thinkers who find their way into intellectual histories, businessmen are usually rather boring. But there is probably a stronger reason for the neglect. For every hour of scholarly research spent on capitalists, I would

---

[16]See Leonore Davidoff and Catherine Hall, *Family Fortunes: Men and Women of the English Middle Class, 1780–1850* (London, 1987).

guess that fifty to a hundred hours have been devoted to finding out how the workers have felt and acted. This is evidence for at least a mild oppositional preference among scholars interested in the making of industrial society.

In the late eighteenth century the industrial revolution became publicly visible with the rapid sprouting of inventor-tinkers. Not surprisingly the first moral issue to plague these men was how to deal with infringement of patents and trademarks. I will begin this account with a few remarks on a very humble tool: metal files (used in grinding, smoothing, etc.) and the difficulties encountered by Peter Stubs of Warrington (1756–1806), a successful and perhaps even distinguished manufacturer of files.[17] In those days before machine tools could turn out machines with close tolerances, files were far more important than they are now. Many machines had to be "touched up" with a file to make them work properly. There were different files for different purposes, and they had to be of good quality.

According to Ashton's account of Peter Stubs and his firm, "the infringement of trade marks is a perennial evil." Other tool makers also suffered from this practice. In 1805 Peter Stubs threatened suit against manufacturers who stamped his initials on their files, although there is no record that he ever sued on account of what looks like blatant fraud. On 2 March 1806 his successor John Stubs offered fifty pounds as a reward for information leading to the conviction of an offender or offenders in another similar instance.[18]

The infringement of trademarks and patents was an obvious attack on property rights. In this particular case, however, the attack did not have very serious consequences. There is no hint in Ashton's account that Peter Stubs could be forced out of business in this manner. The most significant aspect of the whole tale is that some manufacturers engaged in such piracy, apparently with impunity, a good deal of time. Still the infringements look like little more than an utterly dishonest nuisance. In other cases they were more threatening.

The case of Richard Arkwright (1732–1792), if not the inventor of textile machinery, at least the first man to make it work on a large scale and as a major commercial success, stirred up much more public excitement than Peter Stubs and his files. Arkwright's patents threatened the lives of many

---

[17]See T. S. Ashton, *An Eighteenth-Century Industrialist: Peter Stubs of Warrington, 1756–1806* (Manchester 1939).
[18]Ibid., 69–70. See also 60–64 on the importance of such files before the days of standardized parts.

more people far more seriously. Arkwright too was troubled by patent infringement and in 1781 opened his first legal offensive against it. His prosecution failed because, as the defense claimed and the judge and jury agreed, Arkwright in his patent "instead of disclosing his invention did all he could to hide and secrete it."[19] It seems likely that Arkwright did leave the specifications vague in the patent documents in order to forestall illegal copying and the proliferation of unlicensed machinery. (More than one machine was at issue but since this fact has little or no bearing on the issue of patents as uncertain property rights we shall ignore it.) If that was indeed Arkwright's strategy, it was a dismal failure. His mechanical and commercial success generated a host of imitators.

The next major move by Arkwright was a suit against his nearest neighbor, Peter Nightingale, an eccentric sporting squire with business interests and a taste for hard liquor and low company (and who also turned out to be the great-uncle of Florence Nightingale). The suit began on 11 February 1785. Again the key issue was whether the specifications in the patent were sufficiently clear to enable a competent person to build the machine. This time five witnesses for Arkwright claimed to have built a machine based on these documents. This time the jury found for Arkwright (Fitton, 105-113).

Arkwright's victory made his situation much worse. The Lancashire spinners were seriously upset at the prospect that now all of them would have to operate under a license from Arkwright and pay the fees he charged. For this reason they applied successfully for a writ of *scire facias* (do thou make known) to have the verdict annulled. The trial began on 25 June 1785. In about a year Arkwright was forced to concede defeat. His patent was canceled. Once more the issue was the alleged ambiguity of the patent (Fitton, 117–119, 135).

Arkwright's defeat reverberated through the small world of inventor-tinkers. As early as 1781 James Watt, who made basic improvements in the steam engine, Josiah Wedgwood, foremost English potter of his day (d. 1795), and Matthew Boulton, who established in 1769, with James Watt as his partner, the first successful plant for making steam engines, were all distressed by the legal attacks on Arkwright's patent. They feared making improvements that some quirk or writing of the law might take away, as happened to Arkwright. It will be necessary to defend property, one of them wrote, "since there are men who are fools and Rogues enough to invade it" (Fitton, 138–140).

[19]R. S. Fitton, *The Arkwrights: Spinners of Fortune* (Manchester, 1989), 93–98.

Since the examples of Peter Stubs and Richard Arkwright bracket the range of responses to patent infringement in this early period, there is little or nothing to be gained from an examination of other cases. The rather high emotional charge of those defending their patents is understandable from their feeling that they were being unjustly deprived of the fruits of their hard work, not to mention the obvious risk to the capital they had invested in plant and machinery. Patent infringement was also a personal attack, as appears clearly from Peter Stubs's practice of stamping his files with his initials. Counterfeiting those initials threatened Stubs's reputation for high quality.

There was also plenty of moral indignation fed by material interests on the side of those opposed to patent restrictions, mainly the Lancashire cotton spinners threatened by Arkwright's temporary legal victory in the suit of 11 February 1785. The legal representative of the Lancashire spinners took the high moral ground of public and national interest. Arkwright's patent represented a monopoly. Legal recognition of the patent would enable Arkwright, already a rich man, to choke off the livelihood of thousands of hard-working people. Moreover, it would in time destroy the flourishing British textile industry in which England already led the world (Fitton, 119–120, 146, 203).

From the vantage point of two centuries of hindsight the whole issue looks like a great deal of pother about not very much. Despite the loss of patent protection Arkwright continued to prosper. His reputation did not suffer, as shown by the fact that George III knighted him in 1786. The knighthood, however, was not (or at least not ostensibly) a reward for success in business. Arkwright received it in response to a congratulatory address to the king on the latter's escape from an attempted assassination. He made up the loss of his patent protection through his business skill and organizing capacity. Thus he died in 1792 as one of the richest industrialists in eighteenth-century England.[20] At a higher level of generality it is obvious that the concern over patents did not put a spoke in the wheels of the industrial revolution. England went on to become the workshop of the world in the next century. Yet if patent infringement turned out to be a nonissue over the long run, it was *the* live issue for innovating business leaders at the start.

---

[20]See the eleventh edition of the *Encyclopaedia Britannica*, 2:556–557. This edition is justly famous for the high quality of its scholarship and often gives details not found in later sources.

Let us now put the question more broadly. Protecting patents was no more than a means to an end. But what was the end? Did it have any moral component?

Right away we can rule out any notion that making "big money" was the prime motivation of these early tinkers and inventors. It is quite clear that Richard Arkwright thoroughly enjoyed the status, prestige, and comfort that abundant wealth had brought him in his later years. (He had begun his working life as a barber.) The same is true, though with less money, of a well-known contemporary and occasional rival, Samuel Oldknow, about whom there will be more to say in a later context. Both men were happy enough to make money, but that was not what they lived for. One final case illustrates this point because the source explicitly denies the importance of hunger for money. The author of a monograph on Boulton and Watt, the firm that manufactured the first economically useful steam engine, reports that Boulton got himself into a variety of manufactures "in quite a casual way . . . following rather the dictates of an active and restless mind than the immediate motive of a search for profit."[21] That characterization fits very well in what I have called an age of inventors and tinkers.

Let us now pause briefly to see what the meaning may be of these inventors and tinkers, certainly major figures in the industrial revolution according to the classic writers on early capitalism Marx and Weber. Both Marx and Weber present vivid portraits of the early capitalist, stressing the motivation of a historically novel character and personality. Though Weber emphasizes religious history where Marx stresses social relationships as the causes of this new personality, both paint quite similar pictures. The new man was a monomaniac in producing for the sake of production, accumulating capital for the sake of accumulation. In this way, Marx emphasized that the capitalist forcibly multiplied society's productive forces. For Marx of course primitive capital accumulation is a highly immoral procedure. Weber's description is hardly more flattering. His main stress lay on the anxious treadmill-like behavior of the capitalist in his search for a sign of salvation. That in turn, he declared, was a decayed version of Calvinist predestination, a doctrine whereby a few will be saved, the rest sent to eternal torments. While alive no one can know for sure whether salvation or damnation is the fate to be expected. And for that matter there is nothing one could possibly do even if one did

---

[21]Erich Roll, *An Early Experiment in Industrial Organization: Being a History of the Firm of Boulton and Watt, 1775–1805* (London, 1930), 132.

know. (If anyone really did know that salvation awaited him—our problem concerns males—he would have been absolutely unbearably smug instead of disagreeably so, as was often the case.)

The real question here, however, is not how did Marx and Weber explain this behavior, but did the behavior actually exist? Is that the way capitalists, or at least an important segment of them, actually thought and acted? I have found precious few signs of such driven behavior. Such a description fails to make sense of Peter Stubs, Richard Arkwright, Samuel Oldknow, Matthew Boulton, and James Watt, or the contemporary accounts, Andrew Ure, *The Philosophy of Manufactures* (1835) and Alfred [Kydd] *The History of the Factory Movement: From the Year 1802 to the Enactment of the Ten Hours Bill in 1847* (1857). All the men encountered in these sources were hard workers, but it would be impossible to say that they worked for the sake of work and produced for the sake of production. For that matter it is not easy to discern any common motivation toward work in this collection of national luminaries of the industrial revolution. All tinkered with their machinery to make it more reliable and efficient. All did their best to protect the market for their products, a point that will require more discussion later. These two generalizations are hardly surprising and scarcely suggest the frantic monomania suggested by Marx and Weber.

It is of course hardly likely that Marx and Weber invented their early capitalist out of whole cloth to suit their theoretical preconceptions. Here is one description of late eighteenth-century ironmasters in South Wales that at least brings to mind their model.

> Of humble origins (not normally farmers . . . but more commonly from the secondary metal trades) they were often as demanding of themselves as of others; business was their consuming interest and they continued to lead the simple lives to which they had become accustomed *and to which there was little alternative.* [Emphasis added, B.M.] They practiced a stringent personal economy and rigid austerity to maximise their savings. Withdrawing each year from their firms only a small part of the profits for their personal needs, they paid themselves small salaries . . .
>
> The fact that so many of these entrepreneurs were also members of Nonconformist sects reinforced their tendency towards abstinence; hard work and thrift discouraged them from a sybaritic life style or a conscious attempt to ape the upper classes, even when they had made a fortune.[22]

[22]Edgar Jones, *A History of GKN*, vol. 1, *Innovation and Enterprise, 1759–1918* (London, 1987), 46.

There must have been clumps of entrepreneurs like these scattered over much of England (and Scotland) towards the end of the eighteenth century. This evidence does give some support to the classic Marxist-Weberian thesis. Still, their thesis appears quite rhetorically exaggerated.

So far we have been discussing the moral issues facing those early capitalists whose firms attained or in time would attain national stature. When we look further down the scale at provincial capitalists, we find that economic accumulation definitely was not the central purpose of their lives.

For the provincial capitalist "the purpose of business was not the avid pursuit of profit, but the provision of a "modest competency" so that his family could live in a simple but comfortable way." A good many men retired from business as soon as they had achieved a "modest competency" in order to enjoy the fruit of years of work.[23] Put succinctly, business existed for the sake of the household. In these sober circles the cold-blooded pursuit of profit was deeply suspect on moral grounds (Davidoff and Hall, 22).

All the way across the religious spectrum of the day there was agreement "that the home must be the basis for a proper moral order in the amoral world of the market." Men could work in that amoral world only if women's moral vigilance at home was able to rescue them. Once again we see here that division of labor by which the specialist in virtue, usually the priest, enables the layman to sin and society to carry on essential tasks. In this case, however, the division of labor is by sex within the household. Ministers also kept a watchful eye on behavior in the home because every "serious Christian" knew that the home was the one place where the moral order could be sustained (Davidoff and Hall, 74, 89). To the extent that this clerical supervision of domesticity prevailed, early nineteenth-century England appears to have been the first land of the *Sittenpolizei*. Could the reaction against clerical supervision be an important reason for the later remarkable growth of intellectual and political freedom?

---

[23]Davidoff and Hall, *Family Fortunes*, 16–17, 91. This perceptive and penetrating study is based primarily on evidence from Birmingham, a town with numerous small industrial plants and artisan-like shops, and from Essex and Suffolk, areas of arable agriculture. Within these areas the authors collected three kinds of evidence: First, using qualitative material supplemented by a sample of wills they mapped out the relations between named individuals and families. Second, they studied local communities, their physical lay-out, their economic, political and religious profile, and their local organizations. Third, they took a sample of middle-class households. Together it provided a quantitative framework for qualitative information. See p. 34. The body of the work also contains a number of revealing quotations from letters, notebooks, and diaries.

Home, then, was the presumed bulwark against the moral and physical threats of ordinary existence. These included those from continuing political unrest, the moral and physical stresses of acute poverty, brutality, threatening sexuality, disease, and death. Even behind the sheltering walls of the home a middle-class individual of say the 1830's was liable to encounter one or more of these scourges in the course of growing up (Davidoff and Hall, 357). Such evidence arouses the suspicion that home as a moral refuge was in those times more of an ideal than an attainable reality.

How could a member of the middle classes attain the moral bulwark of a home and, more generally, a morally acceptable niche in the social order? The accepted and, to a great extent, also the truthful answer, was by sustained hard work and attention to business. It is important to recognize the historical novelty of this answer. In the preindustrial social order being a member of "polite society" required an independent income, either from land or the city of London. By the end of the eighteenth century this life of gentility without manual or mental work had ceased to be acceptable for many in the middling ranks. The impulse toward change was in large measure religious. Salvation, it was now claimed, was the mark of gentility. An artisan's son who managed to get an education and find a good middle-class occupation could consider himself as much a gentleman as a member of the landed upper class. Later on in the century, as occupational groupings became more distinct, a man identified himself with what he did rather than in terms of kinship and religious loyalties (Davidoff and Hall, 73, 230).

Creditworthiness came to epitomize the desired moral qualities of the businessman as the use of credit became more and more an important aspect of business life despite suspicions and hostilities that survived from an agrarian era. (See Davidoff and Hall, 198 on the distrust of credit.) A creditworthy man was a dependable man, especially in repaying his debts. He displayed all the new—that is, nonaristocratic—virtues of thrift, prudence, and steady application to work. Outwardly he gave no sign of emotionally or financially distracting ties and expenses. His house, furniture, horse, and carriage should be of good quality, indicating solid financial resources, but definitely not showy. Above all there should be no signs of a taste for champagne and sexual variety, at least not in these provincial circles in the first half of the nineteenth century. (Even at the apogee of capitalist hedonism in the Edwardian era (1901–1910) erotic luxury emitted a disreputable odor for many Englishmen, and perhaps especially for English women.) These diversions could swallow up huge resources in a brief time. Besides they under-mined sound and prudent judgment. As representatives of the world of credit, bankers were under especially close public scrutiny and were the ones who felt most severely the self-imposed restrictions of the code of creditworthiness.[24]

Fortunes were changing and uncertain in this early period. Credit ar-rangements in the provinces were local or at most regional. Hence per-sonal reputation was the key to survival. The behavior of the entrepreneur, his family and household, as well as their material setting, all served as indications of financial and moral probity. The two were inseparably linked. Further, the flexibility and relative liquidity of middle-class prop-erties intensified the importance of personal ties in business. The impor-tance of personal connections may have inhibited overly predatory behavior in business. But the web of personal ties also had negative con-sequences. The main source of bank failures, we are told, was the bankers' desire to help troubled businesses, a desire that came from personal friend-ship (Davidoff and Hall, 208, 215, 247). Evidently there was a severe moral conflict between the obligation to help out a friend and the obligation to run a safe and profitable bank. Since banks were not the only source of funds, it is likely that this conflict of obligations permeated business in general.

Just as success in business was taken to be a good indication of moral probity, so was failure in business treated as an immoral act requiring religious censure. For the Independents, a major Protestant nonconform-ist sect, failure in business was a failure in the responsibilities of steward-ship. Goods were held in trust for God, and "nothing but probity will support credit" (Davidoff and Hall, 86). The presumption that some moral failing lay behind each and every business failure could hardly have been attractive to the ordinary man of business caught short by the dis-appearance of a market for his goods or a sudden rise in the cost of labor and/or or materials. Nevertheless there was a moral stigma to bankruptcy through most of the nineteenth century and even later. The religious and moral sanction came into effect through the overlapping of religious and business networks. As noted above, the minister was expected to keep an eye on the personal and business concerns of the heads of families and businesses in their congregation. Moral auditing of a business for its hon-

---

[24]David and Hall, *Family Fortunes*, 247. David S. Landes, *Bankers and Pashas: International Finance and Economic Imperialism in Egypt* (Cambridge, Mass., 1958, 1979), chap. 1 presents a vivid and penetrating sketch of the mores of French bankers at a later date. The essentials of creditworthiness, I suspect, are international.

esty, industry, and competence could result in both the shunning of bankrupts by fellow religious believers and, at the same time, the creation of a class of outcasts in the world of business.

In this world of business, however, religious and ethical considerations did not win out all the time. The Galtons, a well-established Quaker family in Birmingham, had a gun factory directly dependent on the slave trade, whose abolition was a favorite Quaker cause. In 1795 leading Quakers appealed to the Galton conscience without effect. To his fellow Quakers' representations, Galton replied that his main concern was making a living, and that neither the trade in slaves nor the sale of arms implied approval of their use. For some time Galton capital remained tied up in gun production. But the family also took care to diversify.[25]

The middle classes in their world of business formed a major source of the rational and scientific impulse that transformed so much of English society during the nineteenth century. In the early part of the century religion was not yet opposed to scientific thought. Instead religion supported a rational outlook and the active pursuit of commerce. A more significant impulse toward rationality came from the main activities of the middle class: production, design, and building. This rationality expressed itself in a strong taste for measurement and construction of categories. By the early nineteenth century, visitors were struck by the evidence of this passion for exactness: the watch in everyone's pocket, the fetish of using scales for weighing everything including one's own body. Categories became weapons of progress. Rural culture, about which middle-class people often learned from their domestic servants, became the repository of folklore, fairy tales, superstition, and the supernatural. Elements of boisterous play and carnival were separated out as fit only for children and child-like social inferiors. Sexuality, perceived as one of the most irrational forces, was driven back into the core of marriage. Women, especially pregnant ones who were thus incontrovertibly sexual beings, were connected with animal-like nature and hence unfit for the serious work of the world. Categories of purity and pollution, separating the useful from the wasteful, were invoked by scientific and sanitary movements to control noxious materials, sights, sounds, smells — and people. Smells and the absence thereof became an index of respectability and indeed the whole social

[25]Davidoff and Hall, *Family Fortunes*, 88, 102 on religion and bankruptcy, 102–103 on Galton. I have avoided Davidoff and Hall's expression "overlooking" because it could be confusing. Instead I have used "keeping an eye on," "supervise," and "inspect."

hierarchy (Davidoff and Hall, 26-27; see also 383, 399 on the social aspect of smells).

A moral code often gains much of its hold over people as a result of their need to struggle against others with competing codes. Through this competition a group forges its own moral identity by distinguishing itself from other people. As Davidoff and Hall point out in the passage just cited, the English middle classes through their conception of rationality with its emphasis on accurate measurement "sharpened their perceived distance from the easy-going, haphazard gentry [and] the feckless, super-stitious working class." I would only add that the middle classes were fighting off the threat of relative sexual permissiveness that prevailed in both the class above and the class below. In the course of the nineteenth century the antagonism toward the gentry and the aristocracy died down as political considerations, mainly fear of the urban workers, brought middle classes and landed classes together. Hostility to the working classes has remained significant among the middle classes down to the present day.

We have seen that economic success and failure were closely connected with moral standing, but the two were not identical. Wealth did not guarantee high moral standing when it derived from "ill-gotten gains" or was spent in a profligate manner, especially on liquor and women. In this society moral standing in the community evidently had its own indepen-dent criteria, a precipitate of Christian experience. "Good" morals meant above all strong control over impulses and instincts (sex, aggression, food and drink, sleep, enjoyment of beauty). The controls did not reach the extremes of asceticism, though it seems plain enough that Christian as-ceticism was their moral and emotional ancestor. The controls repressed temptation in the interests of economic labor and the search for salvation. All that is reasonably familiar. What matters most in the present context is that their moral code and the controls it imposed gave the middle classes a sense of superiority over the rest of English society—those above and those below—because they could interpret their experiences with mem-bers of the other strata as proof that such persons had inferior moral controls.

Inferior moral controls, or more bluntly, inferior morals, were of course a major charge that many early capitalists leveled against the workers of their day. But there was a great deal more than this familiar accusation in the capitalists' views about their moral obligations—or lack thereof—to the workers. We may now look more closely at how capitalists felt and behaved in their relationships with workers between about 1780 and the 1840's.

Capitalist Morality and the Workers

Before we get down to cases a few words about the imperatives of beginning industrialism are necessary to explain why capitalists and workers, or employers and employees, behaved the way they did. In order to run a factory, capitalists had to recruit, retain, and especially in the early days, discipline the workers. Discipline for the most part consisted of eradicating erratic preindustrial work practices and making the workers' behavior suit the machine with its consistency and accuracy.

Within the framework of these imperatives the moral obligations of the employer to the workers varied from a diffuse set of obligations about the material, moral, and social welfare of the workers and even the workers' families to a narrowly economic duty embodied in the wage contract. The diffuse set of obligations are usually described as patriarchal or paternalist. It includes the wage contract but also a great deal more. The wage contract itself contains more than strictly market determined economic matters. The wages are expected by both capitalist and worker, even if they disagree sharply on the exact amount, to provide enough to live on at a customary standard. The "pure" wage contract was supposed to reflect the demand for labor and supply thereof and be free of extraneous social and moral considerations. The more of these considerations one could get rid of, the lower a firm's wage bill would be.

On the other hand, the capitalists' own interests were enough to prevent the trend towards a pure wage contract from reaching its logical conclusions. Capitalists were nothing if not practical men who certainly could learn from experience, especially disagreeable experience, about matters that affected the work force. Workers dead from cholera, sick from other increasingly preventable causes, or sodden with drink were of no use to an employer. Through these obvious facts a variety of ideas about the employers' individual responsibility and society's collective responsibility (i.e., through government agencies) for the welfare of the work force began to make their way back to intellectual respectability. In the course of the industrial revolution this interplay of historically changing imperatives and responses to them produced a wide range of variation in capitalist ideas and behavior.

Curiously enough the capitalist tinker-inventor whose relations with his workers most clearly anticipate modern trends was also one of the earliest industrial revolutionists, Richard Arkwright.

As early as 1775 he had completed the patenting of machines that would do all the preliminary work connected with spinning by machinery.[26] In other words he had managed to mechanize the whole process of manufacturing textiles. What about the workers who tended these machines?

Arkwright's system of labor relations attracted considerable attention in his own day. From the surviving records it looks like an astute mixture of strict authority, softened by grants of limited autonomy to supervisors and workers, the whole sweetened by high wages. According to one source evidently connected with factory inspectors, it was difficult in Arkwright's day to find people with skill and experience to do cotton spinning. Those who had the knowledge were said to be of "loose and wandering habits," as was often the case with skilled craftsmen in those times (and later). Local people avoided factory jobs because contact with such characters carried with it a loss of status. Arkwright, it is claimed, solved the problem of recruiting and retaining a dependable labor force under these unpromising conditions by imposing strict discipline and granting high wages. Most workers were paid by the piece, not by the week. All workers had the privilege of leaving any moment they chose. It was reported that this privilege produced a steadier and more contented work force than could be obtained with the strictest indenture.

Another area of autonomy existed in the relationship between workers and supervisors. In the works as a whole there were twenty-one rooms or departments, each under the control of a supervisor who had the right to choose his own hands. Correspondingly workers had the right to change at the end of every week and go to any room in the establishment where the supervisor would employ them, provided they gave six days previous notice to the master they were leaving. This informal system of sorting supervisors (called masters and overlookers in the contemporary texts) and workers apparently produced at least moderately congenial groups. In practice there was not much moving about.

The information about just what strict discipline meant in the Arkwright works is rather sparse. Historians and biographers of Arkwright

---

[26]E. Lipson, "Richard Arkwright," *Encyclopaedia of the Social Sciences*, vol. 2 (New York, 1937), 193.

are more interested in his technological than his social inventions. Probably strict discipline meant showing up for work regularly and on time, and paying careful attention to the technical requirements of each job for the number of hours the job lasted. (There were no coffee breaks in those days. But how did they manage a visit to the toilet?) We do know that some of the disciplinary methods which struck other workers as especially unjust were not used at the Arkwright plant. There was no fine or punishment except for damage to the works from evident carelessness. Corporal punishment was never permitted.[27]

The sheer size of Arkwright's "empire" was an historical novelty that impressed contemporaries. In terms of the number of workers employed it was the largest in the country. Soon after the turn of the century it had between 1800 and 1900 workers (Fitton, 146). The large size in itself created a need for novel forms of organization and supervision. What the new social organization had to accomplish—that is, spin as much cotton as cheaply as possible by using machines—was at least equally important in determining the new social organization. Andrew Ure in his *Philosophy of Manufactures* (London, 1835) was one of those who recognized and admired the revolutionary nature of Arkwright's social achievement. The main difficulty to be overcome, he claimed, was not the mechanical one of creating a machine for drawing out and twisting cotton into a continuous thread. Rather it was in getting people to work together in one cooperative unit "and above all in training human beings to renounce their desultory habits of work, and to identify themselves with the unvarying regularity of the complex automaton." The creation of a code of factory discipline that would do just that was "the Herculean enterprise, the noble achievement of Arkwright" (Ure, 15). More specifically, this disciplining of the labor force, as the Marxists would later call it, would put an end to the preindustrial habit of working in alternate bursts of energy and rest. Likewise it would put an end to the skilled crafts with their combination of stubbornness and inaccuracy (Ure, 16, 19–21).

Here, as in other passages, Ure introduces an authoritarian theme that does not appear in the surviving descriptions of Arkwright's system. Ure's contrast between the demoralized poverty of the English countryside, where cash relief was being given on the basis of alleged need without regard to the ability or willingness to work, and the "noble spirit of industry, enterprise, and intelligence" in the cotton factory

[27]All facts about the treatment of workers in Arkwright's works come from contemporary or nearly contemporary sources quoted in Fitton, 205–206.

towns, villages and hamlets reads like a modern conservative indictment of the urban black and Hispanic underclass in the United States of the late twentieth century (Ure, 354–357). In further observations on the moral effects of the factory system Ure stresses the connection between the owner's morality and internal factory discipline. This is a much broader issue than the owner's sexual exploitation of women under his control, though this was and remains a significant issue in its own right. The owner who is generally lax, according to Ure, will soon find that his employees become lax, and the product of his plant second-rate in terms of quality and workmanship. The result is that such an owner gets only second-rate prices and second-rate customers. Any knowledge-able visitor can easily spot such a plant by its general air of slovenliness. If the owner tries to enforce strict discipline, he only makes matters worse for himself because the workers have no respect for him and become angry at the petty vexations of the new orders. True discipline, Ure and many modern authorities hold, means a capacity for delaying self-gratification. The most dependable device for instilling this virtue was for Ure the Christian religion. One of Christianity's main tenets was that life on earth was no more than a frequently miserable prelude to the life eternal after death. Where master and men took this lesson to heart, Ure claims there could be productive harmony and profit (Ure, 415–418, 423–424).

Now we may examine briefly some of the variations on Arkwright's system of labor relations. Peter Stubs, the eighteenth-century file maker, did not have an easy time getting and keeping the skilled cutlers and forgers he required. An effective way he hit upon was to grant the worker a small loan to pay off his debts for beer, bedding, clothes, or rent. Stubs then deducted a few shillings a week from wages until the loan was extinguished. Meanwhile the worker usually contracted another loan. In this fashion workers fell into a state of extreme dependence on their employer (Ashton, 31–33; see also 24–28).

Aside from being degrading to the worker, this arrangement was costly for the employer. Rarely did he collect interest on loans made to workers. Bad debts were frequent. There must have been a lot of time and effort spent in keeping track of trivial sums. Nevertheless debt did secure continuity of service and prevent workers from moving to other concerns (Ashton, 36). At least that is what Ashton claims, and he knew the period. Still, if skilled workers were in such short supply, one wonders why they did not simply abscond to another employer as soon as they had run up a noticeable cash debt. Perhaps they developed some sense of loyalty to an employer who helped them out of an awkward corner, and felt that they might not get as good treatment elsewhere. That, however, is speculation.

Samuel Oldknow was a contemporary of Arkwright and also a textile manufacturer. In his relations with the workers he appears to have been an unusually humane patriarch. Though the workers he needed for making textiles were mainly women and children, who were more patient, dextrous, and docile than male workers, Oldknow went to great lengths to find jobs on his rather large estate for the father. In this way he managed to find suitable work for the head of the family and prevented demoralizing situations where the father lived off the earnings of his wife and children. In contrast to many other factories of the day, the apprentices at Oldknow's works were reported to have been well fed, healthy, and contented.[28]

Evidently Olknow did not feel that material rewards were sufficient to induce the behavior deemed appropriate for workers. A wall placard reproduced by Unwin (p. 198) and dated 1 December 1797 reveals a great deal about human problems the employer faced at the end of the century. The placard begins "Whereas the horrid and impious Vice of profane cursing and swearing—and the Habits of Losing Time and DRUNKE-NESS—are become so frequent and notorious that unless speedily checked, they may justly provoke the Divine Vengeance to increase the Calamities the Nations now labour under." To ward off divine vengeance, Oldknow ordains a fine of one shilling for any man, woman, or child caught swearing; and for absence from work without permission, a forfeit of wages for the hours lost. Fines and forfeits were to go into a box for distribution to the sick.

In this episode we can see clearly the meaning and rationale of paternalism. The employer did play to a considerable degree the role of a parent in encouraging socially desirable behavior. He had to. Without dependability the factory could not function. Oldknow seems to have been relatively mild and understanding in his role of parental surrogate.

He also understood the social source of demoralization and asocial behavior in the destruction of the father's role. Unfortunately, as Oldknow's remedy of finding jobs elsewhere shows, no solution for this problem was

---

[28]George Unwin, *Samuel Oldknow and the Arkwrights: The Industrial Revolution at Stockport and Marple* (Manchester, 1924), 166–169, 173–175.

possible within the limits of the individual factory. It was too expensive. No factory could expect to generate the resources to pay for the creation of jobs that had nothing to do with its own production. That problem on the other hand has yet to be solved in either capitalist or socialist regimes, as even a casual reading of the daily paper reveals. Taxation to support and employ workers in production for which the economy provides no demand is unpopular, while disguised unemployment is wasteful and inefficient.

In the firm of Boulton and Watt, the well-known late eighteenth-century makers of steam engines for pumping out mines and other uses, we encounter another variant of early capitalist discipline. Many of the workers were highly skilled, a type that is hard to discipline because such workers on the basis of experience often know better than the masters what will work and what will not. (Ure misses this aspect of the relationship in diatribes against craftsmen.) Hence it is not surprising to learn that a rather paternalist version of inequality prevailed in this establishment. Discipline was lax but relations with the workers were good. Despite the lax discipline this informal atmosphere enabled the management to obtain very accurate knowledge of each workman's performance. With the next generation and a much larger staff, it was necessary to resort to elaborate statistical controls to get similar information that may not have been as accurate (Roll, 221–222, 252).

The early years of GKN—Guest, Keen, and Nettlefolds, a name acquired in 1900—display an absence of paternalist concern for the workers, which contrasts with all the other cases discussed here. Founded in 1759 this firm began as an iron works that soon expanded into mining. It was located in Wales.

The early managers seem to have been frugal and dour nonconformists. The first recorded episode in labor relations took place in 1810. The price of wheat rose sharply just as a depression struck the iron industry. The response of the owner-manager, John Guest, was to reduce the men's wages. That in turn produced the first strike in the firm's history. Within five weeks the strike petered out as the men, pressed by hardship, drifted back to work at the lower rate. This strike set the pattern for much of the nineteenth century. Sharp movements in food prices or wages produced industrial actions invariably resisted by management. In the absence of a union it appears that the workers as a rule lost.[29]

[29]Jones, *History of GKN*, 1:47.

It took a series of outbreaks of cholera to overcome the antipaternalist and individualist attitude of the management, an attitude we shall examine more closely in a moment. During the first four decades of the nineteenth century management was adamant about the need to make a profit in facing its competitors and refused to accept responsibility for the health of its employees. The 1849 outbreak did produce a shock. However, not until 1853, when a new case of cholera was reported did the new owner-manager, Lady Charlotte, speak about sanitary and cleansing measures. Compared to her predecessors she expressed strong concern for the workers' welfare. Between 1851/1852 and 1866 the death rate fell from 36 per one hundred to 25 per thousand. Nevertheless there was an outbreak in August 1866 that within the space of 58 days killed 115 people. The 1866 outbreak occurred a year after the local Board of Health had been persuaded by another GKN manager to institute a major program of sewer construction. Results appeared in about two years. By September of 1868 55 miles of sewers had been built in the GKN area in Wales, enabling householders to install lavatories for the safe disposal of waste. This measure succeeded in banishing cholera from the GKN area (Jones, I: 119–121).

Thus a socially induced disaster—for cholera was the result of identifiable social conditions and the absence of a policy to correct them— served as a shock treatment to make management accept some responsibility for the health of its workers. It was of course in management's interest to accept this responsibility. As mentioned earlier, management could not run a plant with dead workers or for that matter with workers who were fleeing for their lives. Contemporaries explicitly recognized these facts. In the outbreak of 1854 the local works-manager recorded that there had been twenty-one deaths since Saturday with the disease still spreading. He went on to say "The people are so frightened they are leaving in droves, especially the Irish, amongst whom so far it has been most fatal . . . It is with the greatest difficulty that we carry on the mills and other departments." The death toll in this outbreak was 424 (Jones, I: 119). To repeat, then, objective conditions could and did compel early capitalist employers to accept responsibility for the welfare of their workers. The evidence I have seen indicates that the abdication of this responsibility for the sake of profit and under the flag of capitalist individualism was little more than an aberration.

* * * * *

The histories of individual firms, the main source so far on early capitalist attitudes toward the work force, provide us with precious glimpses of what early capitalists actually did. But these sources present sparse information about how the capitalists perceived the workers and the moral standards (if any) they used in judging and explaining their own behavior as well as that of their workers. Fortunately sources do exist that provide exactly this type of information. In reading two parliamentary inquiries into issues facing both business leaders and the nation, one in 1816 examining child labor and the second in 1833 examining more general issues of economic policy, one can almost hear the business leaders of the day explaining and justifying their policies before a parliamentary committee, in those days a key mechanism for focusing official public opinion.

Though the themes in capitalist arguments do fall into a pattern after extended examination, the first impression is one of diversity. The issue of child labor, topic of the Report of 1816, was of course a "natural" for eliciting moral judgment. In the Report, Josiah Wedgwood begins his discussion with two variations on what we might call the "harsh reality" argument. Harsh reality, so the argument runs, makes it impossible to take effective action against whatever distress is under active public discussion. Short hours of work for children, he states, would be impossible "in a society where the great bulk of persons must earn a living by their labor."[30] Children would be better off, Wedgwood continued in an anti-utopian variant of the "harsh reality" argument, if they did not work at all and instead just played and learned their lessons. But, said Wedgwood, such a condition is unattainable (*Report* [1816], 71–72).

What, then, if anything, can one do? Wedgwood had a ready answer: The "only way of securing the comfort of any people is to leave them at liberty to make the best use of their time and to allow them to appropriate their earnings in such a way as they think fit" (*Report* [1816], 73). This solution was a strictly individualist one. The individual's own efforts within the framework of the market provided the best solution to the problems of poverty. Social action in the form of actions taken by the government, or indeed any agent designated by the society, would not do any good and probably would do some harm. Among business leaders there appears to have been wide agreement on this thesis. The most fa-

---

[30]United Kingdom Parliament, *Report of the Minutes of Evidence Taken before the Select Committee on the State of Children Employed in the Manufacture of the United Kingdom, 25 April–18 June 1816*, vol. 3 (1816), 69–70. Hereafter cited in the text as *Report* (1816).

mous exposition occurs in Adam Smith's account of how the market transforms selfish behavior into socially desirable results. This individualist solution via the market has been one of the most influential insights of modern social thought. As the end of the twentieth century approaches, its influence is very far from exhausted.

Not all expressions of capitalist individualism referred to the market as the alchemy transforming individual selfishness into social good. The most outspoken defender of individualism before this committee spoke from a strictly preindustrial and traditional defense of freedom. A Mr. William Sidgewick, identified as a cotton spinner at Skipton, who had operated a factory for thirty-one or thirty-two years, asserted that the health of the 100 to 120 children employed in his mills was much better than that of children running at large. Later in the session he stated that a Parliamentary Bill limiting children's hours of work was "a loss of the British birthright—that of the control of the parent over the child" (Report [1816], 114, 120). Here Sidgewick was referring to the well-known eagerness of fathers to have their children make supplementary earnings in the factory and the general willingness of the children to accept this arrangement.

At the opposite end of the spectrum from Mr. Sidgewick was a Mr. Samuel Stocks, a cotton manufacturer from Manchester. He stated explicitly and freely that work in a cotton factory was unhealthy for children on account of the long hours of work, the heat of the rooms (often reported to be "as high as 75 degree Fahrenheit," which hardly seems excessive to a modern North American), and especially the dust (*Report* [1816], 253). Indeed this report gives the impression that the evils of child labor had become part of the conventional wisdom of the day. Sir Robert Peel's testimony about the bad effects of factory work on children seems to represent, if not majority opinion, at least the enlightened views of the early nineteenth century. He and others were much influenced by the 1796 reports to the Manchester Board of Health on this topic. Evidently these reports became a charter of legitimacy for criticisms of child labor.[31] The reluctance to do anything about this widely agreed-upon evil is traceable to the widespread belief among early nineteenth-century capitalists that they were operating on a very small margin of profit without room to maneuver and pay social costs.[32] Furthermore if any one employer tried

[31]On Sir Robert Peel see esp. *Report* (1816), 139; and statements by other witnesses, 302–328.

[32]For one expression of this view see *Report* (1816), 167.

to do something expensive, he would put himself at a disadvantage in relation to his competition. On the other hand, a law shortening the hours of child labor—or of labor in general—was more acceptable because all firms would have to pay the social costs. Inefficient ones that could not afford the costs would go out of business, leaving the arena free to the survivors.

Though several employers questioned about child labor at the meetings of the select committee replied in effect that child labor was an evil but an unavoidable one under the conditions of the day, this was not the only viewpoint put forth. Two employers counterattacked by stressing the alleged social benefits of child labor. If obviously biased by self-interest, their arguments are by no means absurd. A Scottish employer, A. Buchanan, claimed that the "habits of regularity" acquired in textile work as a child made these boys preferred employees of tradesmen, joiners, weavers, and the like. Also valuable, according to Buchanan is the "ingenuity they acquire in the works" (*Report* [1816], 10). A silk manufacturer, James Pattison, listed among the reasons for child labor the claim that at an early age "fingers are more supple and they are more easily led into the habit of performing the duties of their station," a blatantly conservative argument, but one that is relevant, though not necessarily acknowledged, in any stratified society. The duties of one's station are not a figment of the reactionary imagination. Pattison added that working in factories was favorable to the morals of young people. "[It] keeps them out of mischief and while they are industriously employed they are less likely to contract evil habits than if they are idling their time away." This too is a sensible observation (*Report* [1816], 77, 79).

In 1833, the Parliament's Select Committee *Report on Manufactures, Commerce and Shipping* extended its coverage much more broadly than had Parliament in the report of 1816 on child labor, and therefore it is somewhat diffuse.[33] For our purposes the main value of the report of 1833 is as a source of employers' ideas, again expressed in their own words, about what makes the wheels of industry turn, and more specifically, about the role and interconnection of profits and wages.

There is no carefully constructed economic theory here, though there are echoes of the prevailing orthodoxy. Instead there is something rather

---

[33]United Kingdom Parliament, Select Committee, *Report on Manufactures, Commerce, and Shipping: Minutes of Evidence, Appendix, and Index*, vol. 6 (1833). Cited hereafter as *Report* (1833).

more interesting, at least for the social historian. For the most part the men who speak to us in this document are employers with substantial practical experience, and a noticeable charge of moral passion. Their words constitute the precipitate of both practical experience *and* moral feelings as they try to make sense of the world around them. They want to explain the difference between good profits and bad profits, what is good and bad for wages. Here, then, we get an insight into the working theories and explanations of the men who pulled the levers of capitalist society just as this society was becoming socially and politically acceptable. Only a year before, the Reform of 1832 had widened the franchise for men such as these.

Early on in the report Lewis Loyd, a banker in London and Manchester, expatiates at some length on healthy and unhealthy profits. One does not have to read far to see that the distinction is a moral one. The habits of trade contracted during the wars with France, Loyd contended, were extremely unfavorable to trade. Speculative, large profits became suddenly possible. These bad habits would have to be unlearned. Nowadays, he continued, the profits of trade were small. Industry, great economy, and the proper proportion of skill and judgment were now both necessary and always successful. (Did the virtues pay off with such regularity?) The present state of the economy, Loyd concluded, was therefore much "healthier" than the earlier wartime one (*Report* [1833], lines 401–413).

Though "healthy" profits were a major purpose of business activities it would be mistaken to infer that businessmen were strict economic individualists with no sense of the public good. Instead the evidence shows that at least some of them had a quite clear conception of the public good: essentially, enough material goods to support a customary standard of living for all levels of the population. Economic individualism working through the market appeared to such employers as the best way to produce and distribute such a sufficiency of goods and services. These ideas appear clearly, if in abbreviated form, in remarks by a retired timber importer, George W. Norman. They deserve quotation: "I think it is the duty of the legislature to act for the good of the nation generally: the good of the nation generally demands that no obstacle be thrown in the way of its wants being supplied upon the lowest terms and that the public burdens should be reduced to the lowest possible point" (*Report* [1833], line 3345). In such a conception of the good of the nation, or the public good, there is no room for the idea of limiting or taxing profits for the sake of the public good. Instead profits are perceived as the necessary basis of the public good. But profits were not the only source of the public good. Some employers expounded notions about "fair wages" or a "sufficiency of wages" as necessary for the public good.

What we find are rather ad hoc explanations of the causes and consequences of low wages and high wages, along with a notion of fair wages. From a slightly different standpoint what we see here is a series of theories about bad wages, which can be either too low or too high, with hardly anything about good wages.

According to a Sheffield manufacturer of saws and steel, Samuel Jackson, there are two bad things that affect wages. One is combinations among workers that push wages up too high. The other is foreign competition which pushes down the standard of living of Englishmen to the level of Continentals (*Report* [1833], lines 2958–2968). Jackson goes on to claim that overly high wages lead to intemperance and then to unemployment, as overpaid workers come to price themselves out of the market. His example is dry grinders, the highest paid and most highly skilled workers within his range of knowledge. They do not live long, because they get dust in their lungs. It does not occur to Jackson to acknowledge any moral responsibility on this account. Instead he dismisses the issue by adding that intemperance is a worse enemy than dust in the lungs. His main point remains that high skills plus combination among the workers in the end produced unemployment (*Report* [1833] lines 2772–2823). At the same time Jackson does present a perfectly clear theory relating the level of wages to the public good. It is a subsistence theory. In his own words, wages "below what a working man can subsist on" can cause distress and make property insecure. A few moments later he elaborates by saying "exist upon comfortably" and draws attention to the differences between what comfort means in England and France.

This subsistence theory of wages is also a theory that defines a fair wage. Was it a normative ideal expressing an unrealized and unrealizable goal, or was it a generalization based on widespread experience? Undoubtedly it was both a goal and a reflection of experience. Only a quantitative economic historian could be expected to judge the importance of each component, and then only if enough evidence has survived, which is unlikely. My guess is that any notion of basing wages on the requirements of subsistence was in 1833 still a pipe dream. The hungry forties were still to come. After about 1850, on the other hand, both the conventional definition of subsistence and the capacity to meet it increased remarkably.

In addition to the cost of workers' subsistence as implied in the subsistence theory of wages, two additional determinants show up in the employers' discussions of 1833. One relates wages to the supply of workers. A spokesman for the select committee suggested that the contemporary distress among English workers was due to the "influx of Irish operatives and labourers." Lewis Loyd, the London banker, replied that he was unaware of any serious effect. There was, Loyd agreed such an influx into Lancashire. But there the "rate of wages is generally rather fair" (*Report* [1833], line 427). Presumably Loyd meant fair from the standpoint of the employers, not necessarily the workers. It was a subjective standard meant to sound objective, judicious, and impartial. Because the effect of the influx of Irish workers produced results satisfactory to employers, Loyd could hardly agree that this influx was a source of major distress.

The second major determinant of wages, as the capitalists saw the situation, was the market price for what the capitalist produced. If the price of iron fell, as was the case at the time, wages had to go down.[34] This viewpoint was probably quite widespread. We have already encountered the crusty late eighteenth-century employer who reduced wages when the price of iron went down at his plant even though the price of food had just gone up sharply. Both determinants, the price of the manufacturer's product and the supply of labor, refer to forces beyond the control of any single employer. One contemporary account of Lancashire in a period of severe unemployment repeatedly stressed the point, which most workers understood, that if the employers could not sell their products they could not pay wages.[35]

Whatever differences there may have been in the perceptions of employers and workers, it is plain enough from the nature of the situation that both parties believed wages were determined by forces beyond the control of any single individual. Nor did these forces display the slightest concern for the suffering of any single individual. They were like the snows of winter and the rain of summer, falling equally on the just and the unjust. Was it in the workings of supply and demand in the market that men first glimpsed the frightening prospect of a universe that behaved according to its own laws of motion without the faintest trace of concern for human sorrows and human happiness? Perhaps. But it was also this same social mechanism, as Marx stressed, that overcame so many stubborn and "inevitable" sources of human misery. Capitalists, and, particularly

---

[34]See the testimony of the iron manufacturer Samuel Walker in *Report* (1833) lines 9525–9531; also the remarks of Samuel Jackson at 2866.

[35]W. Cooke Taylor, *Notes of a Tour in the Manufacturing Districts of Lancashire* (2d ed., London, 1842), 46, 69–70, 101.

English capitalists, were major creators of the modern market. How, then, did they perceive their own creation?

In reports from the late eighteenth and early nineteenth centuries, there are several signs that the notion of a competitive market with free entry and exit for buyers and sellers had a long way to go before gaining general acceptance. Instead the traditional medieval guild practice of de facto property rights in a specific set of customers still prevailed widely. (They have not completely vanished as the twentieth century draws toward its close.) Competitive efforts to attract another firm's customers were regarded as highly unethical, behavior very close to theft.

The extent to which this hostility toward competition is a survival of older attitudes is not clear, because capitalism itself continually generates the same attitudes down to the present day. In general, capitalists prefer assured markets and assured suppliers to the hectic and unpredictable fluctuations in the prices of both that often result from the workings of a free market. For this reason alone we can infer that hardly any capitalist has been a consistent and persistent advocate of the free market. At the same time capitalists have certainly agitated to open up markets, closed or limited for political reasons. In such cases the capitalist was and is looking for more customers. ("Free trade" was for a time the capitalist panacea for all forms of poverty.) Thus, although the free market was obviously a product of capitalism, for the individual capitalist the free market was for the most part forced upon him by forces beyond his control.

Returning to the late eighteenth century we learn that the Sheffield trades, later a source of individualist radicalism, regulated their prices by agreement among the producers. It is no secret that this behavior existed among the important steel-makers, and it seems to have been true of other producers as well (Ashton, 43). The notion of property in customers is quite plain from the way Peter Stubs had to sell his files. But it was the factor or middleman who held the property rights in customers and relayed the customers' order to Stubs, without, so far as possible, revealing an individual customer's identity. Any attempt to intrude on these property rights, especially attempts by Peter Stubs to sell his files directly by traveling about the country, was of course a source of acute resentment (Ashton, 51–53). Similarly in the more significant area of textiles, an agent for Samuel Oldknow, one Salte, who was obviously a pretentious blowhard, writes about the "great injury" of selling Oldknow's goods "very cheap." He is also full of chatter about Oldknow's enemies and spies trying to rival Oldknow by selling better goods at a lower price (Unwin, 64–66). A good deal of this talk reads as though Salte was prodding Oldknow to freshen up his products so they would sell better. Nevertheless using competition as an immoral threat reveals current assumptions about expected behavior in the marketplace.

How did Oldknow's better-known contemporary, Richard Arkwright, cope with the problem of marketing his textiles? The recent very detailed biography of the Arkwrights (mainly about Richard) by R. S. Fitton contains no entry in the index for market, sales, or prices. Whatever information there may have been in the text escaped my attention and could hardly have been salient. In all likelihood, then, these issues were not very important for Arkwright himself. Evidently he put all his energies relating to markets into efforts to secure and protect his patents. They could be expected to have roughly the same result; that is, they would secure a legally guaranteed monopoly and monopoly profits for the life of the patent. Attempts to break this monopoly, were, as we have noticed, regarded as immoral and threatening, not only by Richard Arkwright, but by others in similar positions, such as Josiah Wedgwood. Thus the early individualists about whom we know anything regarded free competition as an unmitigated moral evil.

By 1816 a very different perception of the market, based on classical economics, had come to prevail among articulate leaders in business. From this new standpoint the market appeared as a field of opportunities that enabled the individual to better himself. Political and economic obstacles of commerce and manufacturing, such as tariffs or government monopolies, were from this point of view limits on opportunity that diminished England's wealth and should be eliminated.[36]

At first glance this apparently complete reversal of business opinion about competition and the market seems very puzzling. Closer consideration, however, shows the reversal to be an illusion. Earlier views about the immoral nature of competition reflected the views of employers fearing competition for their own established firms. The statement about the virtues of competition, on the other hand, is advice to workers, and perhaps to small businessmen who might be thinking about starting up a new business. It was a way of telling workers not to count on unions or government help, and small business not to count on old-fashioned priv-

---

[36]See Josiah Wedgwood's testimony, discussed earlier in another connection, in *Report* (1816), 73.

ileges or subsidies. Both the older hostility to competition and the newer advice to stand on one's own feet are perfectly compatible as soon as one takes into account the different audiences for which they were intended.

The 1833 *Report on Manufactures, Commerce, and Shipping* presents still another and quite different set of images of the market under early capitalist industrialization. There is little or no talk about the moral evils of competition and nothing about the market as an arena where the individual can seek his fortune and thereby serve society. Instead there is a series of uncoordinated ad hoc explanations about the movement of prices. The explanations obviously reflect the experiences of individual capitalists. The actors on the stage of the market are not atomized individuals but loosely organized interest groups. Thus the explanations display a good dose of realism despite (or perhaps because of) their uncoordinated and ad hoc character.

If one looks at the discussions in this 1833 report under the index entries "manufacturers," "prices," and "profits" one gains the impression that many, perhaps most, businessmen of that time did *not* see prices as a result of the automatic workings of the market. Instead some identifiable group such as the workers, the government, or the agricultural interest appears, playing an energetic and visible role in setting prices. There is a revealing overtone in this chorus of explanations. Individual character and industriousness, whose praise we have heard so often, will, according to one dour Scottish cotton spinner, not get anybody anywhere if the market refuses to take his goods. Such a man cannot borrow because everyone knows he cannot repay (*Report* [1833] lines 5301–5310). Thus the market relentlessly puts limits on human ambition. Some passages lead to the suspicion that for a good many businessmen the workings of the economy and especially the determination of prices were as opaque, arbitrary, and mysterious as the workings of the stock market seem today to the small investor.[37]

For its clarity and realism the explanation of wages stands in sharp contrast to the vagueness about other prices. It comes from one William Matthews, "extensively engaged" in the coal and iron trade. There is no way of knowing how many businessmen would subscribe to his rather disabused explanation of wages. But the explanation's plausibility and simple empiricism makes a widespread acceptance seem likely. According to Matthews, in a bad state of trade the masters (i.e., employers) try to shift

---

[37]See the entries on prices, and especially the comments by Samuel Gurney, a bill broker, *Report* (1833), lines 185, 278–281, 360–364.

part of the losses onto the workmen by reducing wages. In good times the workmen try to participate in the profits of the masters by obtaining an increase in wages (*Report* [1833] lines 9845–9849).

The absence of any moral judgment in this explanation of wages is quite noticeable. Both employers and workers appear to be behaving the only way they can under the circumstances. A moral condemnation of either the employers or the workers would make as much sense as condemning the snow for melting in the spring. Most noticeable in the case of wages, this lack of concern for morality is characteristic of other sections. Such a deemphasis of morality represents a sharp change in educated opinion, one that was to become dominant in the social sciences as they established themselves in the nineteenth century. But there were sharp limits to this trend. Morality still dominated the discussion of political issues, from the Corn Laws, through the reforms of the franchise, on down to the days of Lloyd George and the last liberal offensive before the outbreak of the Great War. Indeed one can make a good case for the thesis that morality attracted more public attention in British nineteenth-century politics than in those of any other major power before or since. This may have happened because non-moral behavior in England was mainly confined to a specific segment of life: price-setting in the economy. (As a whole, economic activity was not free of moral taboos, such as that against cheating.) While the economy may not have been much guided by morality, there were repeated and more visible attempts to surround politics with the sounds and trappings of high moral purpose. Politics seem to have required even more cant than commerce or industry.

If we look at the economic morality of those below the rank of national business leadership—the ill-defined yet very real "middle ranks" of businessmen—recent research provides some unexpected insights. Victorian men, as we have seen, drew a sharp distinction between the home, the base of virtue and purity as well as a shelter from the pressures of the outside world, and the market, the locus of evil (Davidoff and Hall, 74, 89, 357). Such an attitude of course permitted some relaxation of ethical standards in commercial transactions and the establishment for them of a separate ethic, or nonethic, well expressed in the usual American reply to any suggestion of impropriety: "Business is business." On the other hand, the strength of dissident Protestantism in England helped to prevent the flowering there of the American type of materialism and its worship of wealth. At all levels of business ownership and management in the first half of the nineteenth century there are signs of a fear of money, especially of large amounts of money. For many an Englishman of those days there was something demonic and demoralizing about big money. Easy profits and big profits were thought to be bad profits, as we have seen from remarks made shortly after the Napoleonic Wars. Good profits were small but steady and had to be earned with laborious attention to detail.[38] A cold-blooded pursuit of profit was deeply suspect on moral grounds. Furthermore there was a widespread concern with the pervasiveness of sin: a sense of the self as depraved. Making money, and especially lots of money, was by no means an end in itself. Instead, the goal of all the bustle of the marketplace was to provide a proper and religious life for the family (Davidoff and Hall, 22, 87). Once again, as in Adam Smith's view of the market, vice became the provider and servant for virtue. But in the Victorian synthesis each had come to have its separate locus: virtue in the home, vice and temptation in the marketplace.

This collection of fears led to systematic checking on behavior at home and in the marketplace by ministers and apparently also by friends, neighbors, and business associates. It was not quite the same as modern totalitarian spying because the objects of this moral police-work seem to have known who was doing it. In the area of the market its object was to assure strict honesty. In this respect moral police undermined the distinction between home and market. Business failure was moral failure, an inability or unwillingness to be the trustee of wealth (Davidoff and Hall, 88–89, 102).

The cult of domesticity together with the gentry-aristocratic tradition of the cultivated amateur placed still another barrier in the way of moneymaking as a goal in its own right. Success in the marketplace, though important, by no means wholly determined the individual's status. In fact there was much prestige to be had in *not* working, or more precisely, not working to make money. Positive virtue went with a life devoted to family, friends, home, the garden, philanthropy, science, politics, and religion (Davidoff and Hall, 227). Obviously this kind of life needed the support of a good-sized income, ordinarily an inherited one, supplemented in many cases by a period of genteel earnings in a genteel occupation. The system served to create a set of intellectuals strongly attached to the social order but independent of any particular institution or intellectual fashion. Unlike the situation in the eighteenth century, cleverness became a liability

[38]This attitude apparently lasted until the days of King Edward VII (1901–1910). During that decade for the first and only time it became possible for many big capitalists to enjoy their wealth without the proddings of conscience from within and the threatening mutterings of envy and indignation from below. Perhaps no dominant social class has worked so long and hard for such a brief period of ease.

instead of an asset. Furthermore the theory and practice of a cultivated life served as a brake on the rapid jumps from rags to riches and back again. The cultivated life served as a way station between these two extremes. A comfortable way station, it encouraged prudence in considering both business and sexual risks that might promise ecstatic luxury or threaten degrading poverty. Thus, with a stiff upper lip and eyes ordinarily averted from temptation the officers of the army of progress marched steadfastly into an unknown future.

Dishonesty, Continuity and Change

Our inspection and interpretation of the evidence is finished. What moral changes and continuities do we see in the way of life of commercial leaders during the Middle Ages and commercial and industrial leaders of the industrial revolution?

The most obvious continuity is that of fraud. The main medieval forms included theft, nonpayment of debts, cheating with weights and measures, and misrepresentation of the quality of goods offered for sale. All of these practices still take place today. At the same time there are, of course, obvious historical changes. The development of complex financial institutions in modern times has made possible, and perhaps even encouraged, new varieties of fraud. But in this instance historical change appears to be mainly additive. It is hard to find any form of fraud that has become historically obsolete even though some older prohibitions, such as those on usury and trading on holidays, have lapsed. New technologies on the other hand expand the opportunities for fraud. Railroads to move a much bigger volume of mail at much higher speed were necessary to make mail fraud a profitable undertaking. The modern stock market has made fraudulent dealings in securities possible on a scale much wider than existed at the time of the South Sea Bubble, which "burst" in 1720. The historical record supports a belief that fraud will always be with us as an ineradicable aspect of civilized society. Wherever there is an opportunity to make substantial gains by legally and/or morally prohibited methods, there is liable to be at least a few people willing to take the risk and try it. It takes only a small number of people to get a fraudulent scheme started. If on the other hand the scheme sounds profitable, large segments of the public are likely to try to get in on the act. During the thirty years between 1868 and 1898, that is, well after the heyday of George Hudson, there were spectacular frauds in the City of London and elsewhere. The authors of the *History of Criminal Law* have recently pointed out that there were undoubtedly many shady business dealings, "yet," they add, "comparatively few of the culprits found their way into the courts and prisons." Likewise the addition of several new forms of criminal fraud to the statute book between 1860 and 1914 "did not disturb the downward trend of recorded crime."[39] If the new legislation created more criminals, as seems quite probable, the criminals were not getting caught. Perhaps the existence of new laws satisfied vindictive victims, while the failure to enforce them satisfied powerful criminals.

One of the few fraudulent promoters on a grand scale in the history of British industrialization was the railroad magnate George Hudson. Unlike his American counterpart, the robber barons, he appears as a unique figure, at least on such a scale.[40] But there is another and more important distinction between him and the robber barons. George Hudson was a failure. When his plans failed in 1849, his deceptions came to light and brought him into disgrace. Perhaps there were more American robber barons, and their schemes generally succeeded, because the United States presented a much wider and richer field of temptation and opportunity than did Great Britain. Be that as it may, George Hudson does appear as a model—almost a caricature—of English fraud at the point when industrialization was well under way. Hence it is worthwhile to glance at his methods in order to understand why they worked as well as why they failed.

Hudson was a great optimist. He believed that by amalgamating the patchwork of existing railroad lines and companies he and his associates would be able to reap enormous profits. This strategy was by no means altogether foolish. But he pursued the strategy with little attention to economic detail. Furthermore he pursued it dishonestly, evidently believing that future profits would conceal misjudgments and soothe unduly tender consciences.

George Hudson and his immediate associates pledged the revenues of railroad lines for the extensions and purchases that were part of his plan of amalgamation (Evans, 23–24). This policy put large sums of money

[39]Sir Leon Radzinowicz and Roger Hood, *A History of English Criminal Law and Its Administration from 1750*, vol. 5, *The Emergence of a Penal Policy* (London, 1986), 117, 118.

[40]There are many others of lesser stature discussed in a curious seven hundred-odd page contemporary compilation by D. Morier Evans, *Facts, Failures, and Frauds: Financial, Mercantile Criminal Revelations* (London, 1859, reprinted New York, 1968). The material on Hudson comes mainly from chapter 2 of this book. There is also a biography of George Hudson which contains some sociologically interesting material not found in Evans's work.

into the hands of shareholders. Evidently this money was not used for construction or other economically useful purposes or else was used unwisely and too late. To conceal these transactions Hudson and his associates "cooked the books" until the accounts bore little relation to expenditures and sources of income. At that time such deception was judged less harshly than now. The morals of the day distinguished between a loose corporate financial responsibility and a much stricter standard for individuals.

To keep his strategy going Hudson needed to disburse large sums of money to stockholders and directors. Otherwise they and the public would lose confidence in him, and his whole system would collapse. In this form of pledged revenues this money could come only at the expense of successors and, then, only if the railroads of the future could show improbably high yields. In other words there was really nothing there in the way of productive resources to sustain Hudson's strategy.

By 1847 the basic difficulties became apparent. There were calls for more money and demands for the postponement of some construction. However works in progress could not be abandoned without heavy loss since the productiveness of a railroad depends on its completion. Meanwhile Hudson was compelled to maintain large dividends in order to sustain a high level of confidence. After January of 1845 no account went to the directors that did not come back altered so as to increase the apparent sum available for dividends (Evans, 45–46).

By early 1849 the game was up. Big railroad companies under Hudson's umbrella were committed to heavy capital expenditures as part of gigantic combinations they had been induced to enter. The absorption of capital in these enterprises led to sacrifices by those who had purchased shares at a premium and which were now negotiable only at an alarming discount. Evidently the public had somehow learned that something was wrong. This situation led to a shareholders revolt. Hudson, believing the discontent would pass, resorted to increased misrepresentation. When the report of the directors was read and presented for adoption in February 1849, the shareholders found the accounts less than lucid and appointed a committee of investigation (Evans, 50–52). The committee's findings put an end to Hudson's career as a railroad magnate.

A striking feature of the whole episode is that capitalist and democratic institutions worked successfully in this instance to uncover malfeasance by a man who had come to enjoy very high social status. The capitalist market revealed distrust of his empire building, and the democracy of shareholders was able to challenge and overthrow him.

As a result of his misdeeds George Hudson was disgraced, but not altogether cast out of respectable or even high society. He managed to repay his creditors quite large sums. These acts must have served to soften his disgrace. Nevertheless speculators who had lost out were most vindictive. Evans describes them as willing to hound him to death after having praised him to the skies as the most successful financier of the age. Actually he seems to have been a fair specimen of the financial morality of his time (Evans, 65–68). With his character tarnished but not utterly destroyed, and much of his fortune lost in paying off his creditors, he still retained his seat in Parliament as MP for Sunderland, the position he had gained at the height of his fortune. Attempts to obtain his resignation came to nothing (Evans, 73).

Opportunity and temptation are enough to maintain fraud as a going concern under a wide variety of historical situations. In China, Russia, and Germany where both political institutions and official doctrine were hostile to commerce and industry, fraud played its part in making these carriers of modernization palatable to the dominant classes. New wealth generally corrodes traditional morality. In so-called post-modern society the opportunities and temptation for fraud, as well as vigorous attempts to stamp it out, are matters of common report in the daily press.

The near universality of fraud and the apparent futility of attempts to eradicate it do not warrant the conclusion that it would be wiser and simpler to decriminalize fraud. Civilized societies today, as in the past, have to engage in a great deal of chronically futile repression in order to sustain some semblance of legality and order. If efforts at enforcement ceased, the rest of the population, many of whom break the law in relatively trivial ways, would be worse off.[41]

With a backward glance at the legal history of fraud two features become prominent. The first and most important is a powerful trend toward increasing rationality and, at least in England, increasing fairness. In comparison with the medieval wager of law with its "character witnesses" (more literally fellow oath takers, whose legal influence depended on their social status and number, and whose knowledge of the facts was ordinarily nil) modern legal practice displays far better notions of what constitutes evidence and how to interpret this evidence. The businessman's need for speedy justice acceptable to foreigners as well as himself has undoubtedly

---

[41] According to a recent English survey, 44 percent of those questioned replied that it was "not bad" to conceal a small part of one's income from the tax authorities. See Anthony Arlidge and Jacques Parry, *Frauds* (London, 1985), 16.

played a major part in this transformation. Nevertheless that is not the whole story. Especially in England a great deal of legal change has come about through lawyers talking to other lawyers. These conversations and debates are often the tiny whirring cogs that set in motion the great wheels of judicial change. The second prominent feature of legal history is the large increase in the kinds of behavior classified as fraud in this period as modern industrial society takes hold. According to one standard history of criminal law between 1860 and the First World War several new crimes were created relating to fraud, embezzlement, larceny, bribery, corruption, and similarly disapproved activities. Once again we see how modern industrial society has created new temptations for fraud, while the essence of fraud, deception for the sake of gain, remains the same. There are some clues suggesting that a disproportionate number of those engaged in the historically novel forms of fraud managed to escape the penalties of the judicial system.

Turning now to the ideal character of the businessman, the ways he was expected to feel and behave and often did behave, we find a great deal of similarity between the medieval merchant and the capitalist in the industrial revolution and well on into the nineteenth century. This similarity is somewhat surprising since the industrial revolution was one of the greatest transformations in human history. Still, it may be less surprising if one of the major agents of change remains similar throughout.

At both points in time the businessman was a great respecter of established authority, especially his own. By the nineteenth century the medieval equation of economic and political superiority with moral superiority may have seemed rather less self-evident. But the notion was still widely accepted. Our "betters" were what the word said they were: better in just about every way, a notion that has yet to evaporate from popular consciousness. The businessman was also a man of prudence, even if by the eighteenth century he was an inventor or used the inventions of others. Finally the businessman was expected to restrain impulses and appetites, notably liquor and sex, that could interfere with financial judgment. In a word he had to remain creditworthy.

This observation leads us to a review of the businessman's attitudes toward the market. The market of course existed in medieval London and other cities and towns, although it was very different from the market of early competitive capitalism. Medieval city fathers did their best to control the physical location of markets. They decided what could be sold and where, so as to better control price, quality, and the legality of weights and measures. Controlled markets were the keystone of a policy of social stability that attempted to diminish the material causes of popular discontent. The policy did not work very well because the price and supply of goods were largely set by the guild. A powerful guild often enough found it advantageous to evade controls over the market.

By the beginning of the industrial revolution the medieval restraints on the market had largely disappeared. With the important exception of restraints due to patents, any businessman could enter or withdraw from any market, producing a situation of at least moderately free competition. Such competition, as we have seen, the early capitalists found somehow immoral. But they latched onto the new competitive individualism as appropriate for workers. Capitalists told workers that individual initiative and hard work were the only way out of poverty, for the individual as well as the nation. Combinations and or unions would only make matters worse.

Such was capitalist rhetoric. Practice was quite different. The nineteenth-century capitalists never came anywhere near abolishing medieval social policy. In the first place patriarchal relationships between the capitalist and his employees were still vigorous at the end of the eighteenth century and on into the nineteenth. Many capitalists still recognized obligations to provide the worker with minimal material support. The capitalist was also inclined toward an enthusiastic support of measures to produce moral uplift (which could include injunctions against pilfering) and an end to drunkenness. In other words the capitalists sought sobriety, honesty, and reliability in their workers, virtues advocated by the many Protestant sects of the day. In the second place, the spread of industrialism forced employers to support collective action to reduce or eliminate, in their own interests, hazards to health that especially threatened the workers but were a risk for everyone. Mid-century cholera epidemics are a good example. Thus employees were at no point left to fend completely on their own under a cult of neglect justified by individualism. Instead medieval social policy reappeared in a new guise, to cope with the problems of a new age.

What does the evidence tell us about the new capitalists' motivation to work, especially the moral aspects of their motivation, and about the ways they resembled or differed from their medieval predecessors? Perhaps the most important finding is a negative one. The monomaniac workaholic of Marx and Weber appears to have been a very minor figure. The only swashbuckling entrepreneur (the moving spirit of a more recent historical school) that I came upon, was the great railroad stock swindler George Hudson. Economically he was a failure and socially not quite a pariah.

Others were quite happy to gain wealth and social distinction if matters turned out that way. But their hearts seem to have been in their tinkering. They wanted to make machines work better, which in those days often just meant fewer breakdowns. Many others worked to obtain a "modest competence."

The moral aspects of captalist work comes clearly into view when we realize that business failure was widely treated as a moral failure. From this fact it would probably be an error to regard business activity as somehow a blessed and moral service to humanity. Some English capitalists did express pride in what they did. But the notion of service seems to have been mainly an American one that flourished around 1900 and later. We know that for many nineteenth-century Englishmen business was at the very least amoral and therefore threatening. Hence failure generally meant that a pervasive evil had gotten the upper hand. An odor of suspected or real dishonesty clung to every business failure.

Religious officials, no doubt mainly dissenting Protestants, went to extraordinary lengths in ferreting out and rooting out the dishonesty that might lead to business failure. Local ministers had to keep a close eye on the behavior of the members of their flock for this purpose. We do not know how much information the ministers gathered in this way or what they did with it except in a very general way. Nevertheless it is a sobering experience to come upon this archetype of the infamous communist-and fascist-bloc watcher in the heartland of nineteenth-century liberalism. Since the ministers must have been on the lookout for all forms of moral lapses, it is plain that the apparatus for impulse control in business circles became in the nineteenth century far more extensive and punitive than it had been in the Middle Ages. Partly for this reason the triumphant march of Respectability conquered a goodly segment of the urban workers as well as a large sector of the gentry and aristocracy. Cleverness, wit, and adultery almost vanished for a time from the visible social scenery. For a good many Englishmen and women from all social classes that was as good proof as any of the existence of Progress—especially moral progress.

Austerity and Unintended Riches

What are the social and psychological sources of social move-ments that are committed to (1) equality among their members, (2) com-munitarian ideals emphasizing strong ties of affection among members and a belief in spontaneous cooperation without direction by authority, and (3) austerity in the consumption of physical goods and also in the use or display of comforts and ornaments? In the course of time what becomes of such a movement as it tries to put its ideals into practice? Many but not all of those that have lasted—and I shall limit this inquiry to examples that have lasted for at least several generations[1]—have become quite wealthy. How and why does this change come about, and what are its consequences?

Such movements have appeared several times in human history. One may follow their development in accounts of monastic groups in both Europe and Asia, in reports of the growth of the Quakers, and, with much more illuminating detail, in the history of the Israeli kibbutz. Because the kibbutz is an especially revealing contemporary case, it will receive a dis-proportionate amount of attention.

To begin the inquiry we must try to understand how and why a com-mitment to equality, communitarian ideals, and austerity can become established in the first place, and the emotional forces behind this com-mitment. The chief cause is a rejection of the system of inequality pre-vailing in the larger society. The existing distribution of material goods and social esteem appears to be immoral and unjust and to represent a form of moral decay as well as a decline from older and purer ideals. In preindustrial times religion was the vehicle for this criticism. Among the heretical movements in Europe of the later Middle Ages, the notions of

---

[1] For a good study of ephemeral groups and movements in the United States, see Rosa-beth Moss Kanter, *Commitment and Community: Communes and Utopias in Sociological Per-spective* (Cambridge, Mass., 1972).

equality, community, and austerity were in large measure an attempt to return to primitive Christianity in opposition to the growing secular power and wealth of the Catholic Church. With the beginnings of commerce in the tenth century and later, European society also began to display new as well as threatening forms of inequality. The development was somewhat different under Buddhism. There, monasticism began as an attempt to give collective and institutional form to the Buddha's ideals of withdrawal from the secular world and renunciation of worldly goods and pleasures. From the beginning, however, Buddhism rejected asceticism as too extreme as well as ineffective. Buddhist renunciation carried strong overtones of equality and human brotherhood, especially in the context of the Hindu caste system.[2]

Even the original commitment behind the kibbutz movement had strong religious and quasi-religious elements. In the biggest and most influential branch of the movement this commitment was an uneasy mixture of Zionism and Marxism. The Jews were to prove they did not have to be a "parasitic" people limited to commerce, often petty commerce, and sedentary clerical occupations. They would demonstrate that they could work with their hands, make the desert bloom, become a new rural proletariat, and, by breaking the capitalist link between income and social esteem, create a new form of human society.[3]

The Israeli kibbutz shows some modern traits insofar as many of its early leaders thought of themselves as guiding a movement that could take over and change the world. Quakers, too, may have had some such hopes, though modern literature by and about Quakers has little to say about this trait. In practice the modern movements soon came to embody a form of individual or at most group salvation without any attempt to change human society as a whole or, more precisely, without any attempt beyond personal example. On this score, movements for equality, community, and austerity differ sharply from Marxist movements. The latter put nearly all their energies into trying to change human society as a

[2]On Christianity, see Herbert Grundmann, *Religiöse Bewegungen im Mittelalter*, 2d ed., rev. (Hildesheim, 1961); Lester K. Little, *Religious Poverty and the Profit Economy in Medieval Europe* (London, 1978). A brief but meaty introduction to Buddhist theory and practice may be found in A. L. Basham, *The Wonder That Was India* (London, 1954), 256–266.

[3]For a concise treatment of Socialist-Zionism, with reference to further sources, see Paula Rayman, *The Kibbutz Community and National Building* (Princeton, 1981), 9–18. More specific remarks on the hope to reverse the European pattern of Jewish society may be found in David Catarivas, *Vivre au kibboutz* (Paris, 1983), 33–34. Note also Uri Leviatan and Menachem Rosner, eds., *Work and Organization in Kibbutz Industry* (Norwood, Pa., 1980), 64–65.

whole, while treating the search for personal or small-group salvation as moral and political evasion. Yet, where communists have come to power, we can observe the same kind of dissolution of the original ideals that we find when groups committed to equality, community, and austerity discover that their virtues lead to increasing wealth.

The sources of austerity, which in some instances becomes asceticism complete with a panoply of self-inflicted sufferings, deserve separate comment, if only because such behavior contradicts so many current assumptions about human nature. For the ascetic, to take the more extreme form as the best illustration, the Benthamite pleasure-pain calculus is reversed. The ascetic avoids pleasure and seeks pain. Ostensibly this is a form of moral calisthenics in preparation for a religious goal. The reversal is understandable as a response to living in a world of scarcity where existing privileges are defined as unjust. In addition it makes very good sense to reduce desires in order to cope with scarcity. If meat is scarce, one makes a virtue of going without meat. Simultaneously one can feel at least morally superior to those who do eat meat. The more things one can go without, the more morally superior one feels, and the more time one has to pursue virtue and holiness instead of material goods that merely tempt the body to destroy the soul.

In such attitudes it is easy to see a touch of thinly coated envy. To reject pomp, circumstance, and man-made beauty in all of its artistic forms is also to reject the prevailing system of privilege and its symbolism. With the rejection of art there can, on the other hand, exist a keenly sensitive awareness of natural beauty. St. Francis, it is sometimes claimed, opened Western eyes to the beauty of nature for the first time in our history. The ethical objection to the joy of art is not limited to that found in decoration, gold, and silver. It extends also to the coarser physical pleasures of indulgence in food, drink, and sex. Food and drink were primarily upper-class pleasures in a preindustrial society of widespread scarcity.

Not all of these austere and ascetic sentiments were or are a form of class resentment, a way of making oneself different from people one envied yet despised. They stem also from a widespread fear of tempting fate or of arousing the envy of the gods by the appearance of having too much good luck or undue prosperity. Such fear is also understandable in an age of insecurity and catastrophic natural and man-made disasters, along with continuous grinding scarcity for the mass of the population.

At this point in the analysis our next question becomes, How and why did groups of people committed to the ideals of equality, community, and austerity—indeed outright poverty in some instances—obtain sub-

stantial and sometimes great wealth? In searching for an answer it is helpful to recall that there are only three possible ways for an individual or a
group to increase its store of wealth. One is by taking it away forcibly
from other people, or, more bluntly, stealing. The second way, often hard
to distinguish from the first, is to accept the wealth as a gift in return for
allegedly valuable services rendered, such as increasing the donor's prospects for salvation. The third way is for the group to produce more wealth
on its own. In this case the increase will be even greater if those who
produce goods and services are able to exchange them with members of
the larger society.

The second method, the soliciting of donations, has been a major
source of the wealth of some Western monasteries (particularly of the
Cistercian) as well as of Buddhist monasteries—from the beginning of
their existence. Donations have also been very important for the kibbutz.
The Israeli government and the foreign Jewish community, especially
Jews in the United States, have provided a large portion of the capital
necessary for the kibbutzim to establish themselves and function.[4]

The essential elements in a donation are these. Ordinarily donors are
wealthy and highly placed individuals, great lords, important political officials, and, especially in the case of Buddhist monasteries, prosperous
merchant laymen. Land and/or capital, sometimes in the form of treasure,
are what they give to the monastery or the kibbutz. Sometimes by explicit

[4]Louis J. Lekai, *The Cistercians: Ideals and Reality* (Kent, Ohio, 1977), provides a revealing
account of the history of donations to the Cistercians. The original Cistercian goal had been
to retreat from a corruptive society, to seek land in solitary and "desert" areas, and to work
it themselves with the help of lay brothers. Essentially, they wanted to live on the fruits of
their own labor for the sake of moral purity (pp. 30–31, 65). They did do a great deal of
cultivation in this manner. But from the beginning they also violated their own rules by
acquiring lands with feudal revenues, especially tithes. Meanwhile they managed to gain
exemptions from paying tithes themselves (pp. 48–49, 65–68, 282–284, and further on tithes
293–307). By the fourteenth century the original modest Cistercian farms had grown to
become extremely large estates (p. 72), requiring "professional" management. The Cistercians changed from escapists from the feudal economy to early leaders in the modernization
of the economy. For further information on historical changes in donations, see pp. 16, 18,
75, 286–291, 300–302, 307. In regard to the kibbutz, Eliyahu Kanovsky, *The Economy of the
Israeli Kibbutz* (Cambridge, Mass., 1966), 128–129, shows that the organization was not
economically viable and required economic and organizational assistance from the government and other central authorities. Since the 1950s, he also asserts, the standard of living in
kibbutzim had become divorced from their profitability (p. 135). It became necessary to
subsidize the standard of living in order to avoid increased dissatisfaction and defections.
According to the case study of one kibbutz in Rayman, *Kibbutz Community*, 74–76, Kibbutz
Har could not have been established or been able to survive without containing capital
investment from the Jewish community in Palestine and Jews in the Diaspora. Other private
sources also helped; in 1938 they provided 38 percent of the credit of older kibbutzim.

agreement, but more often by tacit understanding, donors receive in return an improvement in their chances of salvation. Conceptions of salvation of course vary historically. That of the kibbutz is not the same as that of a Buddhist monastery, and Buddhist salvation, an end to the soul's migration from one unpleasant existence to another, is very far from any Christian idea. Yet despite the doctrinal differences there are institutional similarities that are more significant for the purposes at hand.

Organized groups committed to equality, community, and austerity are perceived as professionals in the attainment of virtue and, through virtue, of salvation itself. By perceiving and defining them this way, the rest of society reduces the felt need to practice forms of virtue that may be sociologically as well as psychologically impossible on any mass scale. It is of course not enough just to define the professional in virtue this way. One has to pay them with grants of property. The greater the guilt, the bigger the payments and—in time—the wealthier the professional practitioners of virtue are likely to become. To take root and flourish, a critical morality requires a high volume of felt sin.

Outside sources of wealth in the form of donations and subsidies made an important economic contribution to the survival of these deviant and critical groups, with the possible exception of the Quakers, who seem to have pulled themselves up by their own economic bootstraps. Such donations reflect widespread interest and support among the wealthy and not-so-wealthy members of the surrounding society. Donors wanted to have a professionally virtuous group able to produce and distribute salvation, or at least to talk about it in edifying terms. (In present-day society a great deal of what goes by the name of social science serves a similar edifying purpose.)

Chinese Buddhists were almost entirely dependent on munificent donations. We hear very little about independent economic activity by these monks. To be sure monasteries were frequently located on the unfertile tops of hills and mountains above alluvial valleys where peasant swarms grew China's food. On these elevations the monks often cleared the land to grow orchards and decorative gardens. Economically, such efforts were more than nothing, but not a great deal.[5] In European monasteries and in modern times among the Quakers, as well as in the kibbutz, the religious commitment also led to a strong emphasis on productive labor that in the course of time, and with significant doctrinal and organizational

[5]Jacques Gernet, *Les aspects économiques du Bouddhisme dans la société chinoise du Ve au Xe siècle* (Saigon, 1956), 112–120.

changes, generated very noticeable prosperity. In other words, the latter groups chose to emphasize the third route to wealth, producing many goods and services on their own.

The beginning point in the process of creating and accumulating wealth was plain hard work. Looking ahead, we shall see that the process as a whole generated the principal capitalist talents — or vices depending on one's point of view. But for now let us stick to work. At first the hard work of clearing ground and planting crops was done out of idealism and to serve the new collective, usually set in a remote locality. Another motive was clearly sheer survival, and it is impossible to separate the two motives during the early stage. Very soon, however, hard labor was pushed off onto a stratum of laborers controlled by the collective. The Cistercians used the labor of their lay brothers, apparently without qualms of conscience.[6] For the kibbutz the problem was more difficult. Their Marxism made many members reject the use of hired labor as unavoidably exploitative. Even today this is a sore point among many kibbutzniks. But these scruples were overcome by economic necessity and widespread demand from the larger Israeli society that kibbutzim do something to provide jobs for the flood of Jewish immigrants after World War II. The result was to create a large underclass of immigrant laborers employed by the kibbutzim, usually for jobs in small factories. Though it is claimed that these workers were well treated, they were not allowed to become part of the kibbutz community. Thus the ideal of equality underwent severe erosion.[7]

As work yielded greater fruits and more land, and other capital resources became available for the application of labor, the need arose for managerial talents. Two functions of management became important. One was the administrative supervision of labor. It was imperative to make sure that the right job was done at the right time in the right way in order to maximize production while holding down costs. This was the

---

[6]In the beginning the founders vowed to live exclusively from the fruits of their labor. Not long afterward they decided to acquire landed properties far from human dwellings and cultivate them with the help of lay brothers and hired hands. See Lekai, *Cistercians*, 30–31, 65.

[7]Leviatan and Rosner, *Work and Organization*, 64–75, present a general treatment of the issue that brings out the differences among kibbutzim. Rayman, *Kibbutz Community*, 114–119, is an unusually candid treatment that reveals the role of ethnic differences and class sentiments. Joseph Raphael Blasi, *The Communal Future: The Kibbutz and the Utopian Dilemma* (Norwood, Pa., 1978), 132–134, shows in another case study that the issue can be very troubling even in a kibbutz that utilizes outside labor for no more than 7 percent of its total number of work days and for relatively unprofitable undertakings.

productive function of management. The other was to find market outlets for some of the products of the collective.

The Cistercians developed both functions to a high degree. Their outstanding success as cultivators came about during the twelfth century. It was due not only to the acquisition of large amounts of land and the employment of large numbers of laborers, but also to good planning and effective administration.[8] Under the traditional manorial system, large feudal estates were isolated and virtually independent units. Serfs, handicapped by outdated customs and numerous dues and obligations, were left to their own devices with no large-scale planning or direction. The absentee lord was interested mainly in the collection of customary revenues. To all these practices the Cistercian agrarian system came to present a very sharp contrast. Cistercians worked for themselves, knowing that their faith and life itself depended on the success of their efforts. No matter how many grants of land they received, their total holdings remained under the control of the abbot. Each newly acquired piece of land received individual attention in order to make the best use of its potentialities. In order to manage their extensive holdings the Cistercians developed a system of granges or enclosed units. When the estates had grown too large to be exploited as unbroken units they were divided into parcels of about four to five hundred acres. Then open fields were enclosed, and a few simple buildings put up to house lay brothers, farm animals, and equipment. According to the original rules granges were not to be more than a day's walking distance from the abbey.[9] Even if this rule was not strictly enforced, the system of granges obviously extended the abbot-manager's power in space and intensified his control over daily agricultural operations at the same time.

With the help of these new methods the Cistercians won a distinguished reputation for land reclamation, especially in England. Around 1188 one of their sharpest critics asserted, "Give these monks a naked moor or a wild wood; then let a few years pass away and you will find not only beautiful Churches, but dwellings of men built around them."[10] Thus even their enemies conceded that the Cistercians' managerial skills were adding to the medieval output of goods and services.

A great deal of the monks' managerial talent must have gone into locating market outlets. This happens to be especially clear in the case of

[8]Lekai, *Cistercians*, 282.
[9]Ibid., 295.
[10]Ibid., 297–298.

wine. It is worth noting in this connection that originally monastic rules urged the houses to become economically self-sufficient so that there would be no excuse for trade with outsiders and its attendant distractions and temptations. To the Cistercians, however, a prohibition on trade soon looked like a condemnation to near-starvation and a zero growth rate for the order. Hence the prohibition on trade was soon relaxed.[11]

The choice of wine as an object of trade may have been fortuitous. Founded in 1098 at Cîteaux, the Cistercian order had soon acquired many lands that turned out to be capable of producing some of Europe's finest wines. They included the areas producing Meursault, at least two famous red wines of Burgundy, and a series from the Rhine and Moselle regions. Cîteaux became the foremost producer of quality wine in France, a position it kept until the French Revolution. In the Rhine and Moselle areas the sale of wine always formed the monks' best source of cash income.[12] Wool may have been an even more important item of Cistercian trade in the early days, though there is less information about it. The Cistercians concentrated on producing a very high quality of wool.[13]

With high-quality wool and high-quality wine Cistercian managers would not have needed to put much energy or attention on finding and exploring new markets. The markets were there and waiting. What the Cistercians did have to do was to overcome political and technological barriers to getting their goods to market. In the case of wool they had considerable trouble with lay competitors. On the other hand, the commercialization of the Cistercian economy gained speed from their exemptions from taxes and from the ever-present tolls for shipping goods over long distances.[14]

The Cistercians seem to have regarded the acquisition of riches as a morally unfortunate necessity. Whatever their motives, the results for their reputation are clear. It is too much to claim, in the words of one distinguished authority, that their "accrued wealth robbed the order of all spiritual power."[15] However, powerful contemporaries expressed views not far short of this judgment. In the 1160s the order faced a crisis of prosperity. There was far-reaching criticism of allegedly greedy and grasping abbots and of a pervading spirit of cupidity incompatible with the original

---

[11]Ibid., 310–311.
[12]Ibid., 316–317.
[13]Ibid., 312–313.
[14]Ibid.; on exemptions, 311.
[15]H. B. Workman, "Monasticism," *Encyclopaedia of the Social Sciences* (New York, 1937), 10:587.

ideals of poverty and austerity. In 1169 Pope Alexander III, a great friend of the Cistercians, found it necessary to address a sharply worded warning to the order's General Chapter. It charged that the order had relinquished its "original institutions" and that "those who had vowed to abandon the world and clad in the garments of poverty had decided to serve God, now engage themselves in secular pursuits." In 1214 Innocent III repeated Alexander's charges and his "fear of the imminent ruin" of the order.[16] Even if the tone of the complaints indicates envy as their basis, it is plain that at least the officers of the order engaged in high living. In 1135 the pope had still insisted on simplicity in food and clothing—an insistence which suggests that simplicity was hardly universal—while in some cases providing for abbots and their company a general dispensation from abstinence.[17] For those who could share in it, Cistercian high living was not a source of moral complaint. There were also quite a few who insisted on their share. In 1372 a pope graciously acknowledged thirty casks of fine Cistercian wines. The free flow of Burgundian wines made the annual banquets at Cîteaux in honor of neighboring bishops and clergy very popular. The banquets were also expensive. When in 1364 the Cistercians for financial reasons did not issue the usual invitations, the disappointed clergymen turned to the pope. The pope replied that "these 'meals of charity' had become 'too sumptuous' " and that Cîteaux was justified in holding them only every fourth year.[18]

Thus important products of Cistercian assiduity, managerial talent, and some sharp business practices were good food and excellent wines. These amenities and luxuries served, as they do just about everywhere, to lubricate the machinery of rule, making agreements easier and thereby enabling the machinery to run with somewhat fewer squeaks, creaks, and breakdowns.

Looking back now at the ways in which these deviant and critical groups became wealthy, we can see that the commitment to equality, community, and austerity was in itself a source of the sustained and often intense effort that led to higher productivity and eventually to wealth. Virtue may have not only its own rewards but also some unintended ones. Hard work, however, was not enough—managerial talent also had to be found, with perhaps a touch of unscrupulousness. Administrative experience in running a monastery seems to have been useful in that connec-

[16]Lekai, *Cistercians*, 301–302.
[17]Ibid., 72–73.
[18]Ibid., 316.

tion. Finally, as professionals in the pursuit of a virtue admired and even feared in the wider society, these groups could extract substantial amounts of material support from the wealthier elements in the surrounding society. Let us now examine the extent to which other cases resemble and differ from the Cistercian "model."

The Buddhist monasteries do not require extended discussion. The main difference from the Cistercians was that nearly all Buddhist wealth came from the outside in the form of donations whereas the Cistercians managed to generate substantial wealth with their own resources. But the effects were broadly similar in both cases: a serious undermining of the commitment to equality, community, and austerity. The original Ten Precepts of Buddhism include the promise to refrain from accepting gold and silver. Strictly speaking a monk might own only eight "requisites": three robes, a waist-cloth, an alms-bowl, a razor, a needle, and a cloth to strain his drinking water to save the lives of animalcula it might contain. In fact he came to own much more by the convenient fiction that his property belonged to the order, from which he had it on loan.[19] One good source claims that the conversion of the Indian king Aśoka (died *ca.* 225 B.C.) to Buddhism hastened its decline. The conversion helped to produce a large number of converts. The day of compromise had come, and every relaxation of the old strict morality was welcomed by these converts only half converted.[20] By the time Buddhism had taken firm hold in China in the fifth century after Christ,[21] the old Indian rules against commercial activities were scarcely respected any more. The usual evasion was to turn over precious metals to lay individuals so that they might buy objects of primary necessity for the monks. Or the monks might set the metals aside for use as profitable loans.[22] As early as 558 a Chinese author, apparently himself a Buddhist monk, wrote a detailed report about the "wickedness of the monks and the general decline of religious morality." In educated circles there was always a sense that Buddhism was "rich in worldly goods and had a large following, but it was not succeeding in its own terms as a religion."[23]

---

[19]Basham, *Wonder That Was India*, 281–282.

[20]"Buddhism," *Encyclopaedia Britannica*, 11th ed. (Cambridge, 1910), 4:749.

[21]Arthur F. Wright, *Buddhism in Chinese History* (Stanford, 1959), 51, mentions an Emperor Wu of the Liang who reigned 502–549 and took the Buddhist vows.

[22]Gernet, *Aspects économiques*, 149, 154–155.

[23]Stanley Weinstein, "Imperial Patronage in the Formation of T'ang Buddhism," in *Perspectives on the T'ang*, ed. Arthur F. Wright and Dennis Twitchett (New Haven, Conn., 1973), 273–274.

It is quite clear that Buddhist monasteries became wealthy despite early ethical prohibitions and that the early austere morality largely died out. But it is by no means so clear that wealth was what weakened the monasteries, at least not directly. Instead, the monks antagonized the rulers by competing with them for resources and for power. For doing that the monks were to pay dearly.[24]

Turning to more recent times, we see that the Quakers traveled the same route as the Cistercians: from equality, community, and austerity to prosperity—and again with similar results.[25] The Quakers differed from the Cistercians in at least two ways. First of all, the situation in the surrounding society during the industrial revolution and under advancing capitalism in the nineteenth century was very different from that faced by the Cistercians in the twelfth century. For reasons to be mentioned shortly, the Quakers soon found themselves doing what a great many other enterprising individuals were doing: making money in industry and commerce and gaining thereby social approval. As a people engaged in esteemed behavior and doing very well at it, the Quakers lost a great deal of their cultural and even moral distinctiveness.[26]

Unlike the Cistercians, the Quakers swam with the current of the larger society to the point where capitalist England absorbed them. To use the metaphor a bit more precisely, the Quakers were forced into the part of the current that was moving most rapidly. Until well into the nineteenth century industry and commerce were the main occupations open to the Quakers. Because of their refusal to swear oaths to (the Anglican) church and state, they could not attend the universities. Hence their religious beliefs barred them from the law and the church offices, the main professions of the day. Only science, medicine, and of course business required no oaths, but very few early Quakers chose science or medicine.[27]

The second difference from the Cistercians concerns certain ambiguities and ambivalences in the Quaker attitude toward austerity and money making that were very important in easing acceptance by the new capitalist society. For the Quakers, unlike the Cistercians, advancing prosper-

---

[24]Cf. Wright, *Buddhism*, 60–61.

[25]On Quaker equality and community, see Arthur Raistrick, *Quakers in Science and Industry: Being an Account of the Quaker Contributions to Science and Industry during the Seventeenth and Eighteenth Centuries*, 2d ed. (Newton Abbot, Devon, 1968), 24; Elizabeth Isichei, *Victorian Quakers* (Oxford, 1970), xxiv. By the mid-nineteenth century equality was dead. Anthony Howe, *The Cotton Masters, 1830–1860* (Oxford, 1984), 70, describes the Quakers as a "sect in which the wealthy dominated and from which the bankrupt were expelled."

[26]On this aspect, see Isichei, *Victorian Quakers*, chap. 5.

[27]Raistrick, *Quakers in Science*, 10–11, 42–43; Isichei, *Victorian Quakers*, 147.

ity brought only mild moral conflicts within the order and certainly nothing like the reprimands the Cistercians received from even a sympathetic pope. Though the Quakers set great store by frugality, plain living, and hard work, a major current of opinion among them saw nothing evil in the accumulation of wealth. "By no means did they consider money to be objectionable," asserts one authority; "on the contrary—made rightly and spent rightly money was from every point of view, of the greatest value and usefulness."[28] "Made rightly" meant of course honestly and without taking advantage of a customer, especially of a customer's ignorance. However, there are hints in the literature that in real life Quakers often felt a conflict between their ethics and the familiar adage that business is business.[29] "Spent rightly" meant in effect the avoidance of lavish display, and perhaps also putting aside an adequate proportion of one's income for good works.

Not all Quakers professed such an easy conscience about money. Thomas Shillitoe (1754–1836) and John Barclay (1797–1838) "deplored the spread of wealth in the society and its gradual assimilation to 'the World.' " Shillitoe is described as a shoemaker with a neurotically scrupulous business conscience. Barclay rejected a promising business career.[30] In other words, both men were for their time somewhat uncharacteristic Quakers. Yet they were heard. Here and there one also comes upon wealthy Quakers of Victorian times who displayed more than a few traces of a bad conscience about their wealth.[31]

In connection with these variations in expressed opinions about making and spending money we should glance at the Quaker system of internal moral and ideological controls. Despite Quaker ideals of personal freedom a Victorian Quaker was "under minute surveillance and . . . from the mo-

---

[28]Paul H. Emden, *Quakers in Commerce: A Record of Business Achievement* (London, n.d. [preface dated 1939]), 13.

[29]Raistrick, *Quakers in Science*, 319.

[30]Isichei, *Victorian Quakers*, 23. According to the *Dictionary of National Biography*, ser. 1, 18:108, Shillitoe gave up a position with a Lombard Street bank at the age of twenty-four because the bank sold lottery tickets. I do not presume to say whether that behavior qualifies as neurotic. After a brief stint as a shoemaker he became an itinerant preacher for many years, during which time he managed to obtain audiences with two kings of England, the king of Prussia, the king of Denmark, and Emperor Alexander of Russia. John Barclay, though bearing a name famous in Quaker annals, does not turn up in standard biographical source books, including Quaker ones. There are two brief references to him in Howard H. Brinton, ed., *Children of Light: In Honor of Rufus M. Jones* (New York, 1958), 388–389, 403. From them one can learn the dates of his birth and death and that, on being taken into his father's bank, he expressed doubts about the morality of making money.

[31]Isichei, *Victorian Quakers*, 152–153.

ment his birth note was entered in the Minute Books until the time when his Meeting recorded . . . the details of his burial." Expulsion proceedings reveal the severe sanctions that could be applied for misbehavior and the power of the corporate church over its members.[32] Yet this group discipline over the individual member was decentralized and local. Furthermore, much of the discipline appears to have been the expression of a small group's "public opinion" that was constantly being reformulated through give and take among local members. There was no central authority such as a pope or modern totalitarian leader who could determine which ideas were acceptable and which were not. Nor was there any centrally controlled apparatus to make these determinations stick. In the light of the system of surveillance they had, the Quakers were fortunate in lacking such a central authority.

Reviewing the evolution of the Quaker community we can see how the commitment to hard work, which seems to have arisen from the Quakers' effort to distinguish themselves from both the aristocracy and the drifting elements in the lower classes, in time yielded, under the conditions of the industrial revolution, prosperity and comfort for many Quakers. But it also put an end to whatever equality there had been, imposing a considerable strain on the ideal of the Quaker community. Ultimately their ambiguous attitude toward austerity and money making, together with the absence of a centralized system of doctrinal control, facilitated Quaker absorption into a society beginning to display plutocratic traits. In a pure form the free market is rare.

Let us now see how the Israeli kibbutzim approached their aims of equality and community. Despite the concessions made in the use of hired workers, who are not made members of the kibbutz, the internal organization of the kibbutz remains egalitarian in theory and to a considerable degree in practice. In this important respect kibbutz members have been surprisingly successful in resisting major trends inherent in industrial societies both capitalist and socialist. The kibbutz has broken the link between performance and differential monetary rewards. A high officer of the kibbutz or a highly skilled machinist receives essentially the same income as a member who is unskilled or has become too old to do more than very light work. To be a bit more precise, each household receives roughly the same income, with variations to be mentioned later.[33]

---

[32]Ibid., 139, 141.
[33]Yonina Talmon, *Family and Community in the Kibbutz* (Cambridge, Mass., 1972), 2; Haim Barkai, *Growth Patterns of the Kibbutz Economy* (Amsterdam, 1977), 11–13; Catarivas,

Household income consists mainly of goods and services generated by the kibbutz and distributed free among the members, though more are now being purchased by the kibbutz from the outside. The chief items are food, clothing, and housing. Nowadays a large part of medical care is also free. With the possible exception of housing, these items are fundamentally the same for all members. In a good many kibbutzim the available stock of housing varies from old and undesirable buildings with a few amenities to apartments with all the latest electrical conveniences. In allocating living space, we are told, the kibbutz authorities try to favor need over status. A young family with small children will get more spacious and modern quarters than a distinguished elderly couple with adult offspring.[34] Except for a small amount of pocket money voted on each year as part of the budget, a kibbutz member has almost no discretionary income. However, along with the general rise in the standard of living, there has been a big increase in the possibilities for individual choice. In the early days, for example, everybody wore the same size clothes whether they fit or not. When clothes became soiled, their wearer delivered them to the laundry and took a replacement from the top of the pile in the kibbutz's general supply. This is no longer the case. Kibbutz members can choose their own clothes, whose size and shape can be expected to be a fair approximation of their own. From one obviously prosperous kibbutz we even have a report of a fashion show and the possibility of choosing designer jeans and sport clothes.[35]

Though rough equality of incomes mitigates inequalities arising from other causes, by no means does it prevent them. Two causes are especially important in the kibbutz — and indeed in all but the simplest nonliterate societies: the division of labor and the system of authority that, among other things, coordinates the various activities of groups and individuals so that these activities will after a fashion mesh with one another, enabling people to do their tasks on time in order to make the results useful to others.

The time has long since passed when there was almost no division of labor, when every member of a kibbutz was expected to be able to do just about everything and jobs were rotated to prevent the rise of ine-

---

Vivre au kibboutz, 181–184. For a succinct statement of the meaning of equality for Socialist-Zionists, see Rayman, *Kibbutz Community*, 14. They wanted to break the connection between distribution and the individual's output or social position.

[34]Barkai, *Growth Patterns*, 14, explains that housing is allocated on a points system to take account of complicated criteria in assessing needs.

[35]Rayman, *Kibbutz Community*, 236; Catarivas, *Vivre au kibboutz*, 94–98.

qualities. By the early 1970s, if not considerably earlier, this aspect of the kibbutz ethic had undergone a complete reversal: Being a "cork," that is, floating from one task to another, had become reprehensible.[36] Most members by this time were attached to a specific branch that took care of a specific economic activity such as raising citrus fruit in a production branch, or laundry and cooking in the service branches. This rule of attachment to a specific branch was, we are told, the consequence of collective experience with the division of labor, the need to develop skill and familiarity with a job and skill in performing it.[37] The need to develop skill and familiarity with a task is of course a worldwide source of specialization and the division of labor. With regard to the distribution of goods and services, however, the kibbutz displays certain distinctive features. Whenever a person needs anything—cash, clothes, care for the children—one must ask a kibbutz official for it. Such a situation creates a sense of dependence. The only way to gain some measure of independence is to become a respected permanent worker in a branch. Then one can bargain with the labor official in charge of allocating jobs in order to avoid an unwanted transfer or other disagreeable change.[38]

By now the kibbutzim have developed a quite complex system of authority with a set of officers and committees to manage their affairs. A secretariat that meets weekly is the chief executive organ. It is composed of the main officeholders: the economic coordinator, the labor coordinator, the treasurer, the coordinator of education, and several lay members. Subordinate to the secretariat is a series of committees. These include the economic committee, the labor committee, and committees for education, culture, welfare, and health. Some kibbutzim have even more, such as committees for planning, transport, and even human relations and welfare. This last, according to David Catarivas, has the task of preventing or resolving quarrels among individuals and of allocating housing, refrigerators, furniture, television sets, and the like.[39] For these scarce items there are often long waiting lists. Competition for the comforts of a consumer economy is evidently a source of many of the disputes that this committee is intended to mediate.

The proliferation of officers and committees contrast sharply with the early days when the entire membership gathered in the dining room,

[36]Israel Shepher, *The Kibbutz: An Anthropological Study* (Norwood, Penn., 1983), 55.
[37]Ibid., 43–61.
[38]Ibid., 61–63.
[39]Barkai, *Growth Patterns*, 5–6; Catarivas, *Vivre au kibboutz*, 169–170.

discussed and settled almost all the issues of life in the kibbutz. Large increases in the membership of most kibbutzim,[40] together with a much wider range of economic activities and rising prosperity, have over time put an end to these simple arrangements. Now the kibbutzim have what the economist Haim Barkai calls government by committee. The evidence suggests to me that one should go further and, borrowing a British expression, call the kibbutz a miniature nanny state. For every human discontent there appears to be a committee supposed to take care of it.

As might be expected, the officials do have some sources of gratification that are not available to rank-and-file members. An official in charge of a successful productive operation such as a profitable orchard or small factory—though about this there is likely to be some ambivalence—gains prestige and a relatively wide sphere of authority and responsibility, which are in themselves a source of gratification. Some officers, too, may have highly desirable perquisites, most notably the use of an automobile if their work requires frequent visits to town.

Yet there are several elements in the situation that work to prevent the rise of a closed and oppressive oligarchy. After examining the kibbutz one might even conclude that Robert Michels's iron law of oligarchy must be made of rather spongy iron. The first check on authority is the full-membership meeting that still takes place once a week. As a rule, attendance is low, roughly one member in five. But it can shoot up whenever there is an exciting issue. Officials have to be careful to avoid doing or saying something that will raise a storm in the membership meeting. Criticism is often sharp, and to win by a narrow margin may amount to a vote of no confidence. A second check is the short term of office, two years and sometimes less. However, a good many officials may go back to the status of ordinary member for, say, two years and then be elected to another position. Though I am unaware of specific evidence, it is easy to see that this practice could lead to the rotation of official positions among a small group of old-timers. Even so, there are limits to any possible monopolization of office, since the committee system, which often draws on volunteers, pulls in 30 to 40 percent of adult members in running the day-to-day affairs of the kibbutz.[41]

Probably the most important check on officeholders is the burdensome

---

[40]According to Arthur Ruppin, *Der Aufbau des Landes Israel: Ziele und Wege jüdischer Siedlungsarbeit in Palästina* (Berlin, 1919), 209–210, Dagania (or Degania), widely regarded as the first collective settlement, began in 1909 with seven workers. Its success exceeded all expectations.

[41]Barkai, *Growth Patterns*, 7.

and disagreeable nature of the task. Even full-time officers are unpaid. Whenever anything goes wrong, one or more of the officeholders is liable to get a barrage of complaints. (Jewish culture, for obvious historical reasons, has a rich litany of grumbling and complaint.) Those in charge of consumer services are especially liable to these complaints, though they are not the only victims. Nor are complaints by any means limited to formal meetings of the membership. They also take the form of visits by aggrieved or otherwise troubled members to an official who is at home, trying to relax after a trying day. In addition, a great deal of committee work takes place at night. Finally, to add to their burdens, officials have no real sanctions at their disposal, certainly not punitive ones. They must rely on persuasion, on the public opinion of the kibbutz, and on the conscience of the various individuals in order to get people to do what the officials believe necessary. Thus the labor officer, responsible for allocating manpower to specific tasks, must make rounds of the dining room at supper time in order to persuade members to step into jobs that badly need filling.[42] No wonder there is an increasing preference for eating the evening meal at home! It is an even greater wonder that somehow the jobs do get done.

Despite the continuation of a high degree of equality in the distribution of goods and services, two factors have evidently undermined equality in other spheres of kibbutz life. One is the emergence of a system of authority that concentrates the more important decisions in relatively few hands and, as noted earlier, the rise of specialized economic tasks or occupations as part of a quite clear division of labor. Austerity need not detain us here. It is mainly a feature of past history, left behind with few regrets. But we have yet to examine what has happened to the sense of community and community solidarity. These, too, have eroded. In assessing the changes, one must guard against idealizing a past whose records almost certainly fail to reveal adequately the dissension and contentiousness of life in the "heroic" period.

Some of the reasons for the decline of community spirit were external to the kibbutz, and their effect was to diminish the emotional appeal of belonging to a kibbutz. The attainment of national independence in 1948 eliminated one of the main reasons for the existence of the kibbutz move-

---

[42]Blasi, *Communal Future*, 196. The novel by Amos Oz, *A Perfect Peace* (Tel Aviv, 1982 [in Hebrew]; New York, 1985), provides insight into the tribulations of an aging kibbutz leader with close ties to national officials. Talmon, *Family and Community*, chap. 7, and Catarivas, *Vivre au kibboutz*, 155–176, provide further valuable information on the context of leadership.

ment. Today of course there remains for many kibbutzim the continuous threat of hostile attack. To deal with it the kibbutz has had to devote time and energy to devising an effective military defense, a new element which has changed the focus of communal solidarity.[43] The second major factor was the revelation of the Stalinist terror and tyranny that spread through even "informed" Western opinion after Khrushchev's secret speech in February 1956. This event damaged the socialist element in Socialist-Zionism after Zionist goals had, to a great extent, been achieved. Thus the sense of moral outrage and the feeling that the kibbutz movement existed to pursue a larger goal tended to fade. These were important sentiments sustaining a sense of community and shared enterprise in the kibbutz movement. Moral outrage and shared goals, as we have seen elsewhere, have been important sources for a sense of community in other movements to change the world or escape from it.

Since the early days there have also been many internal threats to the communal tone of kibbutz life. These threats arise out of the very structure of the kibbutz as well as from the forces impinging on this structure. As such, they have been the cause of much lively debate within kibbutzim, whose members seem rather more alert and concerned about what is taking place around them than do ordinary inhabitants of town and village in the United States. Two basic but closely related causes lie behind this series of threats to community. With the improvement in the economic situation of the kibbutzim, domestic and family needs, wants, and concerns began to compete more and more successfully with the collective needs and concerns of the kibbutz as a whole. There has been, in other words, a trend toward privacy and private concerns at the expense of public and collective ones. Some of these tendencies were visible from the beginning. They came into full view by the 1950s, as we can see from the excellent studies by the sociologist Yonina Talmon. More recently one can discern a new individualism barely visible in Talmon's accounts. Buttressed occasionally by psychological jargon about self-actualization, one argument now holds that the kibbutz no longer has the obligation or right to bring up its young members in such a way as to make them good kibbutz material with the proper collective spirit. Instead, the kibbutz should rear the young to make the most of their innate potential so that they will become creative human beings.

The following issues have caused lively discussion about the threats to the survival of collective and communitarian practices; I list them in rough

---

[43]Rayman, *Kibbutz Community*, 91, 196–197.

chronological order, since some debates lasted a long time while others were ephemeral.

1. The issue of the teapot: This story has some of the traits of a legend, though one source describes it as an actual occurrence. In the early days one member of a kibbutz managed to obtain a teapot with which he made tea in his room. This act raised a storm among the membership. "Why doesn't he take his tea sociably in the dining room with other members?" said some. "What will happen to the community if some day everybody goes off alone to make tea in the room?" said others. Finally the excitement died down, and the man was allowed to keep his teapot.

2. The issue of allowing children to sleep in their parents' quarters: Since this issue raised questions about collective care for the children and through that the whole rationale of the kibbutz, it will be best discussed separately.

3. The issue of private television sets for home use: This case parallels that of the teapot. Originally a kibbutz had, as a rule, only one large-screen television set, which was for everybody to watch. With rising prosperity came the demand that the kibbutz buy small sets for home use, which was a very expensive proposal. Despite fears that members would spend too much of their limited free time holed up at home watching television instead of taking part in communitywide cultural and recreational activities, the demand for home sets won out.

4. The issue of eating the evening meal at home instead of in the communal dining room: This choice became a realistic one only after kibbutzim could build blocks of small apartments with adequate cooking facilities. The opponents of eating at home argued that the dining room was the social heart of the kibbutz community and the source of its public opinion. If more and more people ate the evening meal at home, this crucial aspect of kibbutz social life would wither away. Thus this issue, too, resembles the incident of the teapot. Opponents also asserted that supper at home would increase the burden of housework on the women. However, it was the women who were the strongest proponents of taking the evening meal at home. Many of them had found their alleged liberation from the tyranny of domesticity through kibbutz life to be a disappointment. They had ended up doing menial "women's work" any-way—washing four hundred dishes instead of four, as one source put it— while the men continued to perform the more highly valued tasks in the productive sector. Hence the women wanted a brief surcease from the strains of liberation and constant contact with other community members, and an opportunity to show their individual and feminine talents in pre-

paring meals for their own families. By now the evening meal at home appears to be a routine choice with hardly any emotional or political overtones. Meanwhile the dining room remains a very lively social center.

5. The issue of kibbutz support for higher education of members who seek it: With its emphasis on the redeeming virtues of manual labor, especially for the Jewish people and their "distorted" social structure, the kibbutz movement started off with a substantial dose of anti-intellectualism. For a long time, too, kibbutzim could not afford to send young members out for higher education. When that did become possible, the young person went forth with the understanding that the selected course of study would be something useful for the kibbutz, such as an agricultural science, and then that he or she would return to put this newly acquired knowledge at the service of the kibbutz. Quite a few failed to return, which increased the kibbutz's reluctance to invest in higher education. During the 1970s, however, this reluctance greatly diminished as funds became available, and the belief spread that the kibbutz ought to develop the differing capacities and qualities of each individual. Students are no longer limited to subjects that will serve the kibbutz; they may take such subjects as film making, anthropology, and even rabbinical studies, a surprising degree of latitude in the light of the antireligious atmosphere in many a kibbutz.[44]

We may now return to the issue of whether children should be allowed to sleep at home with their parents instead of in the communal children's quarters. Here we see the most significant aspect of the tension between domestic and communitywide concerns.[45] All social movements with a strong commitment to moral and social change have to cope with this tension in some fashion. Monastic movements and the Catholic Church as a whole have tried to eliminate the problem through the rule of celibacy. High ecclesiastical officials, however, have been known to promote the interests of their relatives. Similarly, communist parties when out of power try to restrict the personal and marital relationships of their followers to other party members, though it

---

[44]Rayman, *Kibbutz Community*, 52, 236, reports an actual case of a teapot dispute. For paragraph 2, see notes 45–49. For paragraph 3, Blasi, *Communal Future*, 217; Rayman, *Kibbutz Community*, 237; Menachem Rosner, *Democracy, Equality, and Change: The Kibbutz and Social Theory* (Darby, Penn., 1983), v, 55–56, 127. For paragraph 4, Talmon, *Family and Community*, 74–76, 79–80, 84; Rayman, *Kibbutz Community*, 125–126; Catarivas, *Vivre au kibboutz*, 80–89. For paragraph 5, Bruno Bettelheim, *The Children of the Dream* (London, 1969), 225–226; Rayman, *Kibbutz Community*, 158–159; Catarivas, *Vivre au kibboutz*, 113–114.

[45]This tension appeared with the birth of the first babies to kibbutz parents. Cf. Blasi, *Communal Future*, 29; Talmon, *Family and Community*, 4–8.

seems that these restrictions have somewhat decayed wherever the parties became mass organizations. Communists in power try to capture and stabilize the family for their own purposes. From the point of view of those who use these methods to preserve or extend a movement, none of the devices is completely satisfactory. That, however, is true of just about any political arrangement, and it is certainly true of the arrangements for child rearing in the kibbutz.

The essence of the kibbutz arrangement is the special children's quarters in which, under the care of supposedly professional nurses and teachers, all the children are reared from babyhood to some point short of fourteen years. The children are expected to live in these quarters and spend most of their time there, with only brief (but daily) contact with their parents. There have been two main justifications for collective child rearing. One view held that taking care of all the children in the kibbutz together would free mothers from the tyranny of a stultifying domesticity that restricted their horizons to family concerns. Thus liberated, women would be able to play an active role in communal affairs. The other justification was that collective child rearing provided the best way to form unselfish and cooperative human beings suited for collective living in a kibbutz.

Though both justifications turned out to express exaggerated hopes, collective child rearing, with the children sleeping in their special quarters, has been put into effect in most though not all kibbutzim. It has also worked well enough to survive as an institution down to the present day, but with important modification. The main complaint about the system in the 1950s was a very mundane and quite human one. It was extremely difficult and at times almost impossible for the parents to put a small child to bed in the children's quarters. At best the children would engage in diverse bargaining to persuade their parents to stay a little longer; at worst they would howl. Some would howl while others tried to bargain. Often pandemonium prevailed. But pandemonium at bedtime appears to have been a symptom of more severe problems. The child did see its parents each day. For the child the visit was likely to be a period of affectionate indulgence and escape from pressures to behave and to learn. For the parents, the time spent with their child was an intensely emotional interlude, far more intense than it would have been in the case of, say, a toddler underfoot all day long.[46]

The kibbutz was evidently unwilling or unable to sever completely the bond between parent and child, something that would be very hard to

---

[46]Talmon, *Family and Community*, 94–95.

carry out in a community where membership was voluntary. Hence the kibbutz was getting the worst of both worlds, and especially so in cases where nurses and teachers were incompetent. The situation intensified the demand among young mothers to have their children sleep at home. It is also at this early time that we can discern a rising demand "for more freedom, for the cultivation of individuality, for closer contact among family members," a set of demands that, as mentioned above, has become steadily more influential in the succeeding twenty-five years.[47]

At first economic limitations made it impossible to do very much about allowing children to sleep at home. Adult living quarters did not have space for separate sleeping quarters for children, and according to the prevailing middle-class standards such quarters had to be separate. In time, however, as resources grew, it became possible to build additional bedrooms.[48] Nowadays more and more children in the kibbutzim sleep at home. In this more relaxed atmosphere, free of collective supervision, the child no longer enjoys the undivided attention of the parents. Nevertheless, these children still spend all day in collectives made up of their age mates. And for those over the age of fourteen, the collective takes on even greater importance, presumably as the teenager's peer group.[49]

Thus after all the stormy discussions the sky has not yet fallen. The concessions to private and familial concerns may even have strengthened the social fabric of the kibbutz rather than weakened it. There is a considerable body of anthropological evidence showing that human beings find it hard to endure *either* an intimate private setting *or* one of public visibility and obligation for long periods of time. They need escapes from the public sphere and from the private sphere, preferring to move back and forth between the two.[50] To the extent that this is the case, it suggests that the early kibbutz, with its overwhelming emphasis on the concerns and solidarity of the community, might not have been a viable social form for more than a short time.

Despite concessions to private and familial concerns, the collective organization of the kibbutz still stands. There is still a rough and ready equality of consumption that remains independent of the individual's performance as a producer. Except for household possessions that the

[47]Ibid., 96.
[48]Rayman, *Kibbutz Community*, 234.
[49]Catarivas, *Vivre au kibboutz*, 105–114.
[50]Barrington Moore, Jr., *Privacy: Studies in Social and Cultural History* (Armonk, N.Y., 1984), 41–59.

individual or family may now take with them on abandoning the kibbutz, there is no sign of private property, certainly none in the means of production that remain under collective control. Yet the modern kibbutz is a very different kind of collective, serving very different purposes from those of the early days. As this brief review of the major issues has shown, each of which was eventually decided in favor of familistic or individual interests, there has been a powerful trend toward using collective production to increase the range of possibilities for private consumption. One could call the end result miniature socialism for the consumer society.

Such has been the consequence of the disappearance of the old goals and the gradual fading of the old forms of moral outrage that justified the existence of the kibbutz and were the source of its community spirit. The key question now is whether the kibbutz can produce enough to satisfy consumer demand. Pride in their special way of life and traces of the old contempt for the blandishments of bourgeois society may continue for a while to ease the pressures of demand for late twentieth-century amenities. But if miniature socialism cannot satisfy consumers' demands more satisfactorily than the surrounding Israeli society—an odd mixture of garrison state and shopping plaza—the kibbutz movement is liable to become even more marginal to this society than is already the case.

In all of the cases discussed so far there has been a substantial erosion of the original "critical" ideals of equality, community, and austerity. Increasing wealth has been the main cause of this erosion, though not the only one. Increasing specialization of functions and a growing division of labor that requires command-obedience relationships to coordinate new forms of work have also played their part. Furthermore, and particularly in the case of the kibbutz, we have noticed that human decisions can affect the process of transformation considerably. It is possible for a group or movement to cling to some ideals, for example, equality, if it is willing to pay the costs. This observation shows that it would be an error to consider the transformation as a single trend with a predetermined result. Instead there is a set of possibilities or choices.

One possibility is that a movement may split between those who wish to adhere to the original ideals and those who wish to come to terms with the "real" world for the sake of preserving and extending the movement. Such a split occurred among the Franciscans after the death of St. Francis of Assisi in 1226. The main issues were the prohibitions on using money and holding property. St. Francis's own directives on these issues were ambiguous, probably unworkable, and his leadership weak and shadowy at the end.[51] Historically unique factors such as these may well have played a part in this particular split. But setting such factors aside, one begins to wonder why the record does not display many other similar splits. There is plenty of evidence of tension between "orthodox" and "realist" elements in the movements discussed, evidence not fully recorded here because of lack of space. But no other major split turned up except for the proliferation of sects among the Buddhists.

The Buddhist case suggests a clue if not a complete explanation. If we look at movements like Christianity and Marxism that focus on bringing about a moral revolution in the world at large, we notice of course a large number of splits. For all its emphasis on renunciation, Buddhism, with its doctrine of universal human brotherhood, also carries some of the elements of moral revolution. For the Western moral revolutionaries at least, the Messiah or the Revolution come first. The good society comes next. (Or, as in some versions of Christianity, the good society comes only in Heaven.) Thus, for moral revolutionaries the good society lies in the future, indeed, in a permanently receding future. The movements discussed in this essay, however, are very different. All were attempts to set up the good society here and now. They may have hoped for a total transformation of the surrounding world through the force of their own examples. But it was the example that counted. The rest of the world could wait.

Movements to establish the good society here and now in some remote corner of the existing world are, I suggest, likely to remain rather small. In a small movement, a split is liable to end by destroying the group as a whole. Both "orthodox" and "realist" parties are likely to be aware of this risk. By definition the realists especially are aware of it, and are therefore likely to treat the orthodox with at least outward consideration and respect. If the orthodox are not so blinded by the intensity of their doctrinal concerns that they lose all contact with social and economic realities, they will have some grudging respect for the realists. Hence it will be possible to come to reluctant agreements. In this way small movements can survive—and evolve. But in large movements, with permanently receding goals, the situation favors the emergence of different groups with competing strategies and tactics for reaching this goal. One or more of the dissident or heretical groups can split off without destroy-

[51] For details, see M. D. Lambert, *Franciscan Poverty: The Doctrine of the Absolute Poverty of Christ and the Apostles in the Franciscan Order, 1210–1323* (London, 1961), chap. 3.

ing its competitors — which in many cases it would be quite happy to do — or consigning itself to oblivion.

The importance of human will and human decision appears most clearly in the case of the Carthusian monks, the last example to be discussed and one in which original ideals persisted with very little change. The order was founded by St. Bruno around 1084. Seeking to lead an ascetic life in a solitary place, the monks received diocesan permission to settle in a desolate place in the Alps near Grenoble, called La Chartreuse. Their way of life was austere in the extreme: almost complete silence, no meat and very little food of any kind, simple clothing, and much of the night devoted to religious services instead of sleep. Not for them the life of agricultural entrepreneurship like the Cistercians. Instead, each monk lived in a small house or hermitage, consisting of "a living-room, bedroom and oratory, workshop and store-room," separated from the dwellings of fellow monks. Outside of each hermitage was a small garden plot for the monk to tend. It is claimed that these monks would not accept another square foot of land. There appears to have been very little community life. Most of the time the monks ate alone in their cells, and nearly all of their days were spent in silent solitude, given over to prayer, meditation, and study. The only communal activity, except for religious services and Sunday meal, was a weekly walk of some three hours, where "gentle and frank gaiety" was permitted, but "political wrangles and useless discussion formally prohibited."[52]

Through the centuries this austere life has been maintained with no more than quite minor relaxations down to the present day. The order is fond of the self-characterization "Never reformed because never deformed." Even though there may have been more change than appears in the limited secondary literature, this is a remarkable record of stability and adherence to original ideals. What factors explain it?

One significant factor is that the Carthusians managed to avoid prosperity. When prosperity threatened, they gave away most of their surplus to charity and worthy religious causes. They appear to have maintained their traditional poverty and austerity down to about the time of the French Revolution, and they used this as justification for their refusal to take care of troops or beggars. These they feared as invasions from the outside world. By the time of the revolution itself, however, both their economic situation and their policy had changed. Somehow the Carthu-

---

[52]*The Carthusians: Origin, Spirit, Family Life*, 2d rev. ed. (Westminster, Md., 1952), 42–51, 60–61; "Carthusians," *Encyclopaedia Britannica*, 11th ed. (Cambridge, 1910), 5:432–433.

sians must have acquired very considerable resources, because we read of a weekly distribution of 16,000 pounds of bread and an annual distribution of 2,000 livres in cash to mendicants during the period of the revolution.[53]

If such generosity, the report of which may be greatly exaggerated, was a tactic to avoid revolutionary confiscation, the tactic did not work. Their property was confiscated. Following the Bourbon restoration in 1815, the Carthusians recovered only the barren desert on which their monastery stood and for which they now had to pay rent. In these desperate straits they invented and produced the famous liqueur, Chartreuse. The liqueur became a great commercial success and saved the order. But it is said that the monks did not spend this money on themselves nor have they allowed it to accumulate. Some went for the maintenance of La Grande Chartreuse and the construction of buildings at other monasteries of the order. The largest portion, however, was spent on religious and charitable undertakings all over the world. Thus, it has been claimed, the profits from the liqueur have made no difference at all in the Carthusians' secluded and austere life.[54]

For the avoidance of prosperity, especially in the early history of this order, there existed not only human will but also powerful social mechanisms to give effect to that will. Each chapter of the Carthusians was subject to strong controls from the central authority. One control worked through the Visitors appointed by the General Chapter from among priors of the order. During the Canonical Visitations each monk was interviewed individually. Another inspecting body was the Diffinitory, an executive committee composed of eight members of the General Chapter. It had complete authority over the chapters, seeing to it that no abuse could gain ground. According to a Carthusian source, the repression of an abuse has always been speedy and energetic. Because of the committee and the Visitors, the source continues, fervor and discipline have been maintained.[55] We may also infer that the atomized character of monastic society in this order, in which monks rarely came together and were not allowed general conversation when they did, must have made it unusually difficult for unorthodox ideas to gain a foothold.

For the Carthusians austerity seems to have been a more important ideal than equality and community. In general, these two appear as both

[53]E. Margaret Thompson, *The Carthusian Order in England* (London, 1930), vi.
[54]See "Carthusians," *Encyclopaedia Britannica*, 11th ed. (Cambridge, 1910), 5:432–433.
[55]*Carthusians*, 66–68.

the consequences of austerity and instrumental to maintaining it. For their adherence to their ideals the Carthusians have paid a very heavy price. They are now close to extinction. As of the early 1970s there remained only 440 members throughout the world.[56]

On the basis of evidence reviewed in this essay we may now state provisionally the range of apparent possibilities for a commitment to equality, community, and austerity. If the commitment leads to prosperity, as it frequently does, the most likely result is a general erosion of all three commitments. But this result is not inevitable. As the kibbutz demonstrates, it is possible to break the link between pay and performance, thereby maintaining a substantial degree of equality in consumption. This can occur even when austerity is sacrificed. There is also a sacrifice of efficiency and some loss of community in grumbling and confusion about the performance of necessary tasks. The interesting question is whether equality too may undergo alteration with an increasing emphasis on the importance of satisfying the varied needs of individuals. It is too early to tell. Equality has already been breached by the division of labor, including the introduction of hired labor, and by the development of a system of leadership and authority. And the kibbutz as a whole may not be viable without external subsidies.

Finally, as the case of the Carthusians shows, an organization can maintain a high degree of austerity over a very long time. Rank-and-file Carthusian monks evidently lived under a regime near equality in regard to food, clothing, and shelter. But they have been subject to the authority of their superiors exercised through a very strict discipline. Community in the sense of strong mutual ties arising out of spontaneous cooperation in the performance of self-chosen tasks appears always to have been weak or absent. The long survival of the order, even if small in numbers today, in something like its pristine state appears to stem from the rejection of prosperity, encouraged by a strong central authority working on an atomized social order. More succinctly, equality of austerity could survive because of the absence of community and the presence of authority. Thus survival in the case of both the Carthusians and the kibbutz has been bought at the price of a substantial sacrifice of original ideals, as in the kibbutz pattern, or the near absence of at least one of these ideals in the first place, in the Carthusian pattern.

Attempting to peer into the future one can assert that the commitment

---

[56]"Carthusians," *New Columbia Encyclopaedia*, 4th ed. (New York, 1975), 468.

to equality, community, and austerity will arise again and again as long as human societies continue to present felt injustices. But whenever these ideals are put into practice, they undergo a sea change. The end of austerity is morally expensive, its survival morally and economically even more expensive.

Liberal Prospects under Soviet Socialism: A Comparative Historical Perspective

This chapter presents the text of the Inaugural Lecture for the W. Averell Harriman Lecture Series delivered at Columbia University on 15 November 1989, and repeated at Harvard with some minor changes on 8 February 1990. Thus the lecture antedates the formal collapse of the Soviet Union and other exciting historical events. Had such events not occurred, had there been a relatively peaceful transition toward a liberal capitalism with an improving standard of living for much of the population, the interpretation in this lecture would seem not only dated but absurd. Its main interest now, some ten years after it was first drafted, rests in the attempt to discern the forces favorable and opposed to the establishment of liberal democracy on the basis of both western and Asiatic experience.

At the outset a few words about comparative history may tell the reader what to expect and, perhaps more important, what not to expect in this essay. The procedure starts with an issue or problem, which I will state in just a moment. The next step is to search out other societies that have faced roughly the same problem and find out how they coped with it. Comparative history can suggest unexpected answers to familiar questions and, on occasion, show that accepted answers are very likely to be wrong. In this essay I present a substantial amount of comparative history, which I hope is intrinsically interesting as well as appropriate and useful. In emphasizing what *not* to expect, I will add that I have kept comments on recent and current events in the USSR to a minimum. While following and interpreting the rush of current events can be a serious and valuable intellectual task, it is also a highly specialized one. Neither comparative history in general nor this writer can bring to bear the up-to-the-minute knowledge this task requires.

I

The problem I wish to address here is this: Is there any prospect at all that the Soviet Union may acquire or develop the characteristics of a liberal democratic state? Even if one dismisses such a prospect as utter fantasy, in order to be intellectually responsible one has to have good reasons for the dismissal.

The key characteristic of liberal democracy for the purpose at hand is the existence of a legitimate and, to some extent, effective opposition. To put the point in somewhat different terms, ordinary citizens must have rights of remonstrance and criticism against unjust acts. The right and opportunity to complain is very important. It will remain so as long as human societies exist, because every human society necessarily imposes many frustrations on the wants and instincts of the individuals who make up the society. A great many of these frustrations are necessary to make any society work. In this sense they are just and necessary. Others are simply oppressive and repressive. The mere fact that some rules are necessary easily opens the door to oppressive rules and practices that the dominant authorities put in for their own special advantage. Hence the need for a legitimate opposition is a permanent one.

By no means are all social needs satisfied. Some are not even recognized for long periods of time. Many political systems have seemed to flourish even during the twentieth century without internal criticism or legitimate opposition. For that reason we can say that such an opposition clearly marks off liberal regimes from authoritarian and totalitarian ones. In Western democracies legitimate opposition has taken the form of openly organized and competing political parties. For us it is hard to conceive of legitimate opposition in any other form. Nevertheless for the time being it will be best to leave open the possibility that other forms might develop through a process of trial and error.

In assessing the prospects of liberal democracy in the USSR there is the strong risk of setting up an idealized model of Western democracy and then juxtaposing this model against the current workings of the Soviet regime to demonstrate from the lack of fit that liberal democracy is impossible there. I am conscious of this risk and wish to emphasize that the models of liberal democracy I have in mind are the actual working ones. One should keep in mind Churchill's remark, "Democracy is the worst possible form of government—except for all the others." In order to avoid a Western parochialism, in the next section I shall sketch some aspects of both Western and Asian institutional history that may enable us to discern both obstacles to liberal-democratic development and ways of overcoming them. After that I shall discuss some general preconditions for liberal democratic rule and for any possible transition in the USSR.

To begin with Western developments, there are two general points worth making. First, revolutionary violence, and/or civil war, prepared the way for liberalism and later democracy in the three main centers where these institutions first grew up: England, France, and the United States. This violence severely weakened institutions and social groups opposed to these trends. After the execution of Charles I no English king tried to rule without Parliament. The French Revolution dealt a crippling blow to the monarchy and the aristocracy. In the United States the American Revolution put an end to what limited possibility there may have been for foreign domination. American social and political questions would not be decided in London. The Civil War was more significant in that it put an end to the possibility of a slave-owning plantation aristocracy as a crucial segment of the elite. In this connection it is also worth noticing that defeat in the Second World War played a very similar role in promoting liberal democratic regimes in West Germany, Italy, and Japan. The revival of parliamentary democracy since the war is not limited to these countries. It is not always an edifying spectacle. But under close examination no political system turns out to be edifying.

The bearing of these historical observations on the Soviet situation is reasonably clear. If violence on any large scale is necessary to uproot the Soviet elite, then there is almost no prospect for change. Conceivably such a crisis—or the threat of such a crisis—could galvanize a section of the bureaucracy to sacrifice many of its followers in order to create a new social order with new policies, as happened in Meiji Japan. Such a sequence of events is still speculative, though there have been hints pointing in this direction.

II

The second and from our standpoint more important aspect of the growth of Western democracy is the difficulty of creating a system of legitimate opposition. This difficulty I shall discuss with some comparative historical examples. After all, the very notion of a "loyal opposition"—to use a British expression—looks on the face of it like a contradiction in terms. How can one possibly be loyal to the powers that be and at the same time oppose them? Putting the question this way highlights the central puzzle of a long historical process: how could opposition become legitimate, that is, politically and socially acceptable?

In England, as in other countries that have developed a system of legitimate opposition, the main line of political development has been from violent conflict over men and measures to negotiated settlement of the issues. The height of conflict in England occurred with the execution of the king in 1649. No subsequent British king attempted to rule without Parliament, as had Charles I. Thus regicide contributed to the creation of legitimate opposition. But by itself, killing the king was not enough. Many other things had to happen.

First of all, the passions and excitements of the Civil War and Glorious Revolution (1688) had to die down. Life had to become more boring before a civilized political order could begin to take hold. By the 1720s with the last flickerings of the Jacobite party, the excitement had died down.[1]

At about the same time legitimate political opposition started to take shape. As early as 1731 the expression "Opposition" had become current in contemporary writings.[2] At this point and for a long time afterward Parliamentary opposition was a loose agglomeration of place-hunting factions that were out of power and rent by conflicting views and principles. On the other hand, their numbers and advocates outside Parliament included some brilliant speakers and writers who covered their somewhat sordid motives with intellectual éclat. In practice the Opposition at this stage does not appear to have had any other end in view than making trouble for Robert Walpole (d. 1745). As England's first de facto prime minister, he had managed to put together a working government out of a set of turbulent magnates, in large measure through favors and corruption.[3]

This limitation of its objectives is very important in making Opposition legitimate. It was reasonably plain to all who cared to look that a motley body of place hunters had no real intentions of upsetting the political and social applecart. After all, members of the Opposition came from the same

---

[1]Archibald S. Foord, *His Majesty's Opposition, 1714–1830* (Oxford, 1964), 76, 82–92. J. H. Plumb, *The Growth of Political Stability in England, 1675–1725* (London, 1969), 13, puts the end of violence in 1715.

[2]Cf. Foord, *Opposition*, 154–155.

[3]Foord, *Opposition*, 154, 158. Plumb, *Political Stability*, is the main source for my comments on Walpole.

background and were part of the ruling class in a highly inegalitarian society. Furthermore an attempt to revive the passionate atmosphere of the Civil War would hardly have been popular at any level of society.

Over the years the members of Parliament developed an etiquette for limiting conflict. Once more, the fact that all of them came from the upper reaches of the social order and shared at least some measure of political responsibility as an elite within the governing class probably facilitated the creation of this etiquette. The first concrete sign of this emerging etiquette that I have come upon appeared in 1741 when the Opposition was tightening its ranks in a successful effort to oust Walpole. A major Opposition leader is described as having frowned on private friendships between political enemies, a clear indication that such friendships existed. In fact the same leader went on to say that amicable association between courtiers with any bloc of the Opposition aroused suspicion among other elements in the Opposition. Indeed contemporary evidence suggests that friendly relationships among political enemies were not uncommon.[4] That is hardly surprising since political alignments in those days were continually changing. At the same time it was possible for a distinguished political leader to believe that such friendships threatened political purity and ought to be stopped.

Fortunately this attempt to create a social gulf between political enemies was a failure. During the rebellion of the American colonies, Lord North, who was trying to carry out King George III's policy of military suppression, was frequently the target of caustic oratory by Burke, Fox, and others. But Lord North did not let such attacks get under his skin or at least pretended not to. Anecdotes collected after his death claim that his natural civility and good humor left him no enemies in the House of Commons. Even leaders of the Opposition counted on these qualities to the point where they frequently petitioned him as First Lord of the Treasury for little favors and indulgences for their friends and constituents. These Lord North readily granted when he could do so with propriety, acts which his opponents readily acknowledged.[5]

Parliamentary business did not always proceed so smoothly. On occasions of high political excitement speakers on both sides were shouted down by their opponents. (Hooting at speakers still takes place today.) Toward the end of the American War of Independence tempers flared and several duels were arranged on account of "hard words" spoken in

---

[4]Foord, *Opposition*, 206–207.
[5]Ibid., 358.

debate. Though the presiding officers of both Houses did their best to prevent bloodshed there were two celebrated duels, one in 1779 and another in 1780. (Charles James Fox took part in the earlier one.) After the second duel there was a strong reaction in the House. If public questions were to be decided by the sword, said one speaker, free discussion would cease and Parliament would resemble a Polish diet. Another advised his fellow members bluntly to learn "better manners." Evidently the members took this surge of disapproval to heart, for these violent episodes ceased.[6]

By the late eighteenth century, then, the Mother of Parliaments had put in place an etiquette for limiting violent factional conflict within its walls. Now that we have uncovered the way in which legitimate opposition became established, there is no need to attempt a synthesis of all the political maneuvers and other conditions that eventually resulted in the modern system of legitimate opposition. Instead I will end the discussion of the British example by calling attention to two themes: Parliamentary relations with the monarch, and the manipulation of elections.

In the eighteenth century, and of course for a long time afterward, the sticky point in politics was to persuade the monarch to accept as ministers the men Parliament believed to be appropriate under the circumstances. There was not a great deal of difficulty under Walpole because Walpole enjoyed the confidence of George II. Furthermore Walpole, unlike some of the other leaders of the day, knew which of George's mistresses was the one to whom he should appeal in case of trouble. Under George III the situation was very different. His domestic life, it is claimed, was pure, and he was stubborn in defending his prerogative of choosing his own ministers. He was also quite lucky, as shown by the upsurge of electoral support for the Court in 1784, only a year after the final British defeat in the unpopular attempt to crush the American Revolution.[7]

If George III and other monarchs were lucky in not having to swallow too many unpalatable pills of the Opposition, their luck was supplemented by careful political manipulation. It is easy to forget just how effective this manipulation was, but the evidence for it is overwhelming. Between 1742 and 1830 the government always won general elections, mainly through the use of patronage.[8] Eighty-eight years without losing an election is an odd record for the Mother of Parliaments, and longer than even the Bolsheviks can claim to date. As one looks back over the

[6]Ibid., 357–358.
[7]Ibid., 398–400.
[8]Richard Pares, *King George III and the Politicians* (Oxford, 1953), 196.

English record, what stands out is the role of corruption and good manners in establishing the legitimacy of opposition.

In the United States, our next example, during the period of patrician rule by the founding fathers, opposition was generally defined as malevolent factionalism. To be sure, one current of opinion associated with Madison regarded parties as an unavoidable evil that reflected human nature. Yet even there, party and faction were seen as evil, and the terms "party" and "faction" at times seemed interchangeable. When the Republicans were in power under President Jefferson, many of them spoke of their opponents, the Federalists, as incipient traitors.

According to Richard Hofstadter, this situation changed rapidly during the lifetime of Martin Van Buren (1782–1862), who was president from 1837 to 1841.[9] The old patriciate had been men of substance (and intellectual distinction) for whom politics was both an avocation and an obligation. By Van Buren's time this social type had died out. Professional politicians, men like Van Buren who devoted their whole lives to politics, replaced them. Many were lawyers accustomed to pressing cases against their opponents. Such partisanship was, however, both temporary and narrowly focused.

Both as lawyers and as politicians they were accustomed to rubbing shoulders with opponents around the courthouse and on other social occasions. The lawyer's loyalty was to the legal profession and the courts rather than to a particular cause or client. These changes in the social role and situation of the politician made it easier to encapsulate hostilities and to treat political opponents as men who might at some time be useful allies, and with whom it would be prudent as well as pleasant to remain on good terms personally. These changes in the politician's role and social context were important in creating a climate of acceptance for political parties and other aspects of the specifically American variant of legitimate opposition.

There are two more cases that require at least brief consideration. They are important because they are Asian rather than Western. One comes from contemporary Japan. The other comes from Imperial China, mainly the Ming Dynasty (1368–1644). The Japanese case is a success story, and the Chinese one a failure. To the extent that it is possible to explain both with a set of handmade intellectual tools fashioned mainly from Western historical experience, we may have greater confidence that we are asking

[9]Richard Hofstadter, *The Idea of a Party System: The Rise of Legitimate Opposition in the United States, 1780–1840* (Berkeley, 1969), 214–219, 223–230.

the right questions for understanding any society, including the Soviet Union.

One consequence of Japan's defeat in World War II and the subsequent American occupation was the grant to the lower house of the Diet of law-making powers. These powers were similar to those possessed by the House of Representatives in the United States. The consequences at first were nearly catastrophic. They were sufficiently serious to make Western observers dubious about the prospects of democracy ever taking root on Japanese soil. Two apparently irreconcilable blocs formed in the Diet. One was the Liberal Democratic Party, actually a conservative group whose base was farmers and businessmen. It possessed around two-thirds of the seats and, by using questionable parliamentary techniques, could force through legislation sought by a generally conservative cabinet and bureaucracy. The Japanese Socialist Party was the opposition and commanded roughly the remaining third of the seats. It was a leftist party, based in the trade unions, that also appealed to critical intellectuals freed by Japan's defeat from the stifling authoritarian chauvinism of the war and prewar years. The Socialists suspected the conservatives of trying to reintroduce the old regime. The conservatives saw the Socialists as a Marxian-liberal Trojan horse out to undermine the bases of traditional Japanese society. To me it seems probable that both suspicions were basically correct. Because the Socialists could not hope to carry through their program in the Diet, they adopted tactics of confrontation and obstruction to prevent the Diet from passing conservative legislation. The conservatives responded to confrontation with similar acts of their own. The situation deteriorated to the point of physical battles between members of the Diet. By 1960 the Diet seemed close to paralysis.

Instead of disintegrating, however, the Diet pulled itself together in a process analogous to that which took place in the United States and earlier in England. Confrontational politics frightened a good many members of the Diet. Both conservatives and Socialists began to seek each other out to search for issues on which they might agree. This they did secretly at first, meeting in tea houses and geisha houses. Later they did so openly by bringing to life the Diet's system of committees which had lain dormant and unused during the period of confrontation. In the committees both sides learned the limits of what they could hope to accomplish or prevent and how to compromise for the sake of achieving their objectives. By working together each side learned what would wash with its opponents and what would not. Mutual respect put in an appearance. Together the members of the Diet were creating through trial and error a new social role for themselves with a new set of sanctions and expectations. Their emphasis was on compromise and the acceptance of opposition as a legitimate aspect of governing. Simultaneously the opposition muted its demands for an overhaul of the whole society. By the 1970s a new situation had come into existence. Though still precarious and showing signs of creating its own new problems, such as sharply increasing government deficits due to the decline of conservative influence, the new situation showed much promise for the future.[10]

The Chinese Empire throughout its long history had a special governmental institution, the Censorate, especially charged with some of the functions modern Westerners associate with legitimate opposition.[11] As a working institution the Censorate can be traced back at least as far as the first imperial dynasty, the Ch'in (221–207 B.C.), which unified the country by force of arms. The idea of criticizing a ruler and remonstrating with him if he ignored or damaged the people's welfare is very prominent in the surviving texts of the predynastic classical philosophers Confucius (ca. 551–479 B.C.) and Mencius (ca. 372–288 B.C.).

The main functions of legitimate opposition in the Chinese Empire were (1) remonstrance with and criticism of higher officials, including, in theory and occasionally in practice, the emperor himself and (2) surveillance in the sense of seeing to it that the emperor's decrees were carried out in practice by local officials, and (3) of keeping track of popular needs and sentiments. It would be hard to maintain that keeping track of popular needs was an important task all the time. Still, "good" and powerful emperors generally decreed a local remission of taxes when they learned about a bad harvest or natural disaster. After all it was good policy to limit hunger, discontent, and riots. A "bad" emperor with an empty treasury—which might not be altogether the emperor's fault, though concubines and palaces ran into money—would refuse to remit taxes and insist on building new and more magnificent palaces. This he would do against the advice of officials who were telling him the people were starving.

The main weapon that put some teeth in the function of legitimate opposition in the Chinese empire was impeachment. Naturally the weapon could not be used against the emperor himself. Changing em-

---

[10]The material on Japan comes from Ellis S. Krauss et al., eds., *Conflict in Japan* (Honolulu, 1984), 243–293.

[11]For this section I have drawn mainly on Charles O. Hucker, *The Censorial System of Ming China* (Stanford, 1966).

perors required violence in the form of a rebellion. (There were, however, several of these in Chinese imperial history including one at the beginning and another at the end of the Ming dynasty.) Though the functions of remonstrance and surveillance were sometimes separate, they tended to fuse, and they were fused under the Ming. As the way of changing emperors by rebellion makes plain, the Chinese conception of opposition lacked one feature that has become prominent in the West only recently. As a working autocracy China lacked any notion of a "responsible" opposition that could be expected to step in and govern with a somewhat different program and a somewhat different set of people. Too overt and consistent opposition implied serious risks to life and limb. About all an embryo opposition could do was wait for the reigning emperor to die and hope for the best from the next one.

The Censorate worked well under a "good" emperor when it was hardly necessary. Under a "bad" emperor it was almost completely ineffective. Either the emperor disregarded its findings and admonitions or punished severely those who reported matters about which he did not care to learn. At least that was the case under the Ming and probably other dynasties as well. In that sense the Censorate was a failure, and the reason is not far to seek. The Censorate, like other bodies of scholar-officials, had no political base outside the imperial system. Or perhaps one should say almost no political base. When an imperial system began to disintegrate from misrule, popular discontent due to economic hardships, and finally the threat of rebellion and/or foreign conquest, large segments of scholar officialdom would withdraw allegiance because the reigning emperor had lost the Mandate of Heaven. Then they might support one or more candidates for the throne. The emperor, in other words, could not govern without the support of his officials. But this withdrawal of support was a weapon of last resort in a situation of general collapse. In the meantime the emperor could dispose of individual officials as he chose.

III

Let us now examine some of the possible implications for Soviet politics that this historical *tour d'horizon* suggests. In what follows I shall attempt to do two things at once: extract some broad generalizations from the historical material and comment on some aspects of Soviet affairs in the light of these generalizations. According to strict academic logic one is expected to draw the generalizations first and *then* show their application.

In my judgment that is a caricature of scientific method, as well as a dependable recipe for boring readers.

Stalinism of the late 1930s rather obviously represents an extreme variant of the malevolent factionalism and bitter infighting among political leaders just described in English, American, and Japanese developments. It was fortunate for many Soviet citizens that in the end Stalin did not turn out to be immortal. Thus the brute historical facts of Stalinism and tsarism apparently confront us with the question: how can one create a system of legitimate opposition for the first time?

The historical record shows that the problem is far from new. Other states have done it. Nevertheless to create a system of legitimate opposition for the first time is a long, difficult task in which the participants are by no means sure of what they are doing or want to do. Once one state has created such a system, however, others can copy and adapt it. Indeed, within limits, the system can be exported to a society with very different traditions and a very different culture.

Two factors are evidently important in establishing a viable system of legitimate opposition. The leaders of the more important political groups or movements must have, or develop, the sense that they are in the same boat, to sink or swim together. To put the point in slightly different language, most leaders have to recognize that circumstances force them to get along or revert to political paralysis and then anarchy. I say "most leaders" because there is usually political space to let a few intransigents cry their wares in the wilderness. On the other hand, if more than a few of the leaders are intransigents and are forced to remain that way for fear that others will outbid them for popular approval, the result could be situations like those in Lebanon and Northern Ireland.

The other factor is the development of social contacts among the contestants that are, or can be made, distinct from the business of resolving partisan issues. Shared experiences based on social class or professional and economic occupation can aid such social contacts. Alcohol can lubricate them despite the well-known fact that alcohol releases aggressive tendencies. Perhaps alcohol works because it also encourages indiscretion. In any case the effect of these social contacts is to defuse partisan intensity, encourage congeniality and even mutual respect, all of which increase the prospect of what William Graham Sumner used to call "antagonistic cooperation." He thought that that was the only kind of human cooperation worth discussing.

Finally it is possible to set up a system of legitimate opposition *de novo* and by royal decree, at least if it corresponds to widely respected ethical traditions, as was the case in Confucian China. Favorable and deep-rooted ethical traditions like those of Confucian China were, on the other hand, not enough. Indeed they were politically worthless when serious conflict occurred. In this sense a system set up only by royal decree and dependent on royal favor just will not work. If there is to be effective criticism of royal power, the critics must have a social and political base independent of that power. Shifting the scene for a moment to Europe under Western feudalism, we see that such was the situation of the great and often turbulent nobles of those centuries. Despite all the turmoil and bloodshed they caused, modern Western freedoms owe a great debt to these nobles.

IV

Now that we have extracted what we can from the brief historical case studies of legitimate opposition, I will mention four kinds of economic and social conditions widely believed to favor democratic and liberal regimes. (The number four is of course somewhat arbitrary.) It will not do to consider these conditions as preconditions or prerequisites for liberal democracy, because there are liberal democracies that have managed to survive without one or more of these conditions. Nevertheless if we find that two or more of them are absent or weakly developed in a specific case, then the prospects of democracy are dim in that country.

The first condition is a wide diffusion of property among the population. This wide diffusion is important because it provides a social base for independence from the government, as well as from other organized groups in the society. The rise of modern industry and of big government has greatly narrowed the diffusion of property in almost all of the advanced areas of the world. Industrial workers have jobs rather than property. So do white-collar workers and even an increasing number of professionals such as lawyers, doctors, and natural scientists who work in and for large firms or the government. To some extent skill has replaced property as a source of independence. A person with the right skills has a high degree of independence from the employer of the moment. Nobody can take away a skill in the way it is possible to take away property. On the other hand, a skill can become useless very quickly because of technological change. In a socialist society without individual property in the means of production, skill becomes just about the only source of independence. As far as I am aware, no one has yet done a monographic study of this situation in the USSR.

Along with a fairly wide diffusion of property, and now skill, one usually thinks of an economy in tolerable working order as generally necessary for democracy. This second condition is obvious enough to require very little comment. An economic system that deprives a substantial part of the population of its sources of livelihood, such as through unemployment in the case of wage earners and the loss of property in land by farmers and peasants, will cause a great deal of suffering and bitterness. At some point there will be a loss of political allegiance.

There remain two more conditions: (1) The society needs a homogeneous population in which the same culture is widely shared. One can turn this one around by asserting that strong religious differences and ethnic loyalties make trouble for liberal democracies. It has become obvious that they are already creating serious difficulties in the Soviet Union. (2) Political issues in a democracy cannot be too highly charged or too divisive. They cannot become matters of life and death or, more accurately, matters that arouse intense moral passion. Santayana caught the essence of this point through exaggeration when he observed that in a democracy all political questions have to be trivial questions. Are the issues facing the top Soviet leadership in any sense trivial?

There is an obvious subjective element here. What is a highly charged issue, say a tax on salt, in one society may be a trivial matter in another. The emotional charge of an issue depends on social context and cultural traditions. Political agitators can do a great deal to increase the charge. On the other hand, it is very difficult to defuse an issue after popular excitement has been aroused. In the case of the Soviet Union today this is rather obvious. The leadership in order to survive needs to make life both more boring and more satisfactory for the mass of the population. That is precisely what is *not* happening.

V

With the major conditions affecting the growth of liberal democracy before us we may now examine in somewhat more detail how some of them apply to the Soviet Union. You may recall that the first one had to do with the wide distribution of property and the growth of a professional class, or in somewhat looser language, of a bourgeoisie. In discussing the rise of democracies in general one can claim with only slight exaggeration: no bourgeoisie, no democracy.

To what extent does this apply to the USSR? A distinguished authority reports that in 1959—that is, in Khrushchev's time—there were only 5.5 million Soviet citizens with higher education. By 1986 there were 24 million. Within the group with higher education the "bourgeois" core would be those labelled "scientific workers" in the official Soviet figures. The number of these scientific workers rose from 1.5 million in 1950 to 15 million in 1986.[12] These are quite impressive increases even if we have to remember that *any* increase looks big when the starting-point is small.

Some qualitative observations may help to make sense of these figures. First, the entire educated elite is ultimately dependent on the state, though the factor of skill must mitigate that dependence in a way difficult to generalize. In addition the generational difference within the elite may be the most significant fissure. On the one hand, there are the old bureaucrats who want to sit with folded hands and take life easy, as an old Soviet saying has it. Then there is the younger, better educated group that takes many of its cues and tastes from advanced Western societies, especially the United States.

To bring about a democratic and liberal transformation the economy must of course be in reasonably good working order. That is hardly the case in the Soviet Union now. Consumer supplies are short and the lines waiting for them very long. Such is the situation more than seventy years after the revolution and more than forty years after the end of a devastating war. It is not easy to see just how *perestroika* is expected to correct this situation. But it is not hard to see what has to be done and that so doing will create a host of powerful enemies for Gorbachev or any leader with a serious commitment to economic reform. It will be necessary to set up a series of positive incentives and negative sanctions to put ginger into economic administrators. Subsidies will have to be sharply reduced. Plant managers will have to stop taking last year's targets with a minimal increase for the current year as their basis for their operations. They will have to innovate and improve the quality of their products. The same kind of ginger will have to be applied to workers. Absenteeism will have to be reduced, and discipline improved. Above all they will need better machines to work with, the main key to raising the productivity of labor.

In a phrase, Schumpeter's "gale of destruction" will have to sweep through the Soviet economy. The gale can get its force either from the acts of economic planners or from letting loose the forces of the market,

[12]Gail W. Lapidus, "State and Society: Toward the Emergence of Civil Society in the Soviet Union," in Seweryn Bialer, ed., *Politics, Society, and Nationality: Inside Gorbachev's Russia* (Boulder, Colo., 1989), 126.

or some uneasy combination of the two. But gales are destructive. No one wants to be exposed to their force. When, or rather if, the gale begins to whistle, all sorts of administrators and workers can be expected to come forth with all sorts of reasons why their special preserve of economic turf should be spared the rigors of reform.

If the economic situation is unfavorable, the ethnic and cultural one is scarcely any better. The Soviet Union is far from a culturally homogeneous society. There are numerous national minorities with cultures very different from the dominant Russian one. Unlike the situation in the United States, most but not all minorities inhabit a distinct territory in the form of a republic. The separate territory can encourage nationalist and separatist movements. Clearly there is quite a bit of political tinder in the national republics. Socialism has not quenched it. However, a Hapsburg policy may in this case succeed. Barring an overall crisis the Russians may continue to stay in control as long as each national minority gets angry about a different issue at a different time. They are divided already. So all one has to do is rule.

VI

This review of the conditions necessary for, or favorable to, liberal democracy and their applicability to current Soviet conditions leads to quite pessimistic conclusions. Still it would be a mistake to end the discussion here. Important political trends do not necessarily cease to work themselves out just because they encounter obstacles. The trend toward the unacknowledged goal of some variant of liberal democracy shows enough momentum to make worthwhile an assessment of some problems in any attempt at transition.

The best way to begin such an estimate of these admittedly formidable problems is with a reminder: there has never been anywhere such a thing as democratic socialism firmly in power. When democratic socialists (or perhaps better, social democrats) gained power temporarily through the ballot box, their commitment to democracy, along with other considerations too complex to summarize here, has limited the changes they were willing to make in the social fabric and therefore enabled their opponents to defeat them. Where Leninist socialists have come to power by revolution or civil war, even if they began with some commitments to democracy, they found it necessary to discard such commitments or twist them into new shapes. Leninist parties were minority parties committed to a complete overhaul of the society they had conquered. To control and later to mobilize the population they had to create from unpromising sources a series of huge bureaucratic apparatuses. Roughly speaking, administrators, propagandists, and policemen made up the apparatus as a whole. The striking and intriguing feature of the Soviet case right now is the clear awareness in high political circles that this bureaucratic mobilization has performed its historical task and has become obsolete. By now the bureaucracy so created has turned into a major threat to the welfare of the Soviet population as well as to the international standing of the USSR.

After this reminder the first question to ask is "who, if anybody, wants liberal democracy in the Soviet Union?" Though there is little solid information on this point, the most likely answer is that nobody wants it for its own sake except a few intellectuals. In general, people have not wanted democracy for its own sake or out of commitment to a political ideal. For the most part those who have actively sought democracy—in the literal sense of rule by the populace—have wanted it as a device to increase their share in political rule and weaken the power and authority of those who actually rule. Democracy has been a weapon of the poor and the many against the few and the well-to-do ever since it surfaced in ancient Athens. The liberal component, where it has existed, was an attempt to gain protection against arbitrary acts by *either* the poor and many, or the dominant few.

Can one find anything in the current Soviet scene that at least resonates with liberal notions of protection against arbitrary acts by rulers as well as ruled? The obvious answer is yes. Plans and statements of intention have been appearing in the press at an astonishing rate. They are welcome to anyone with a strong moral commitment to liberal ways of resolving social problems. The fact that they sound promising from this standpoint provides no justification by itself for the "crack-pot realism" that would dismiss these statements as mere window dressing.

Glasnost, or openness and candor, a very old Russian tradition, is of course the most familiar aspect of current Soviet democratic aspirations. Since events tumble after one another so rapidly in the USSR, it is impossible to do them justice here. I can only say that they not only *seem* extraordinary but *are* extraordinary to both scholars and journalists.

Aside from the fact that candor and openness is an old tradition among educated Russians, appearing in almost every nineteenth-century novel, and as a result therefore seems to be independent of any political system, there is only one other observation I can offer. From a comparative historical standpoint the enthusiasm for things Western, now loosely associated with glasnost and Gorbachev, is a phase that a segment of the educated elite in various parts of the world frequently has gone through at some time. Here we may recall the early Meiji oligarchs who took Herbert Spencer seriously, or Sun Yat-sen's blend of Marxism, democracy, and nationalism, or reformist efforts offered by the educated elites of Bengal. To a modern skeptical eye these phases look rather like a case of the intellectual measles. Even so, Gorbachev's bold attempts to apply glasnost to all parts of the USSR do stand out as a new historical phenomenon. The novelty appears in Gorbachev's political agility and astuteness, bolstered by a liberal-democratic emphasis among many of his supporters. He is trying to use democracy to draw the teeth of a sclerotic bureaucracy. Differences and quarrels we can expect to see, but in a brief essay we cannot discuss them.

Gorbachev is on record as being opposed to a Western type of multiparty democracy. Though he almost certainly means what he says, it would be unwise to take his statement literally. If he, or anyone else, wants to make socialism more efficient and more humane, where *can* they turn except to the Western tradition? There is much talk now about giving the masses a greater voice in economic and political affairs. Much of this talk may be pure eyewash. We have heard it all before. One has to ask "whose masses" and "what are they expected to want?" Nevertheless it would not be surprising to find some populist and democratic appeals used to chip the rust off some bureaucratic machines.

What would a socialist version of liberal democracy look like? We could work out an answer, I suggest, by extending current trends toward their logical conclusion and by taking seriously the democratic aspects of their own tradition. Self-criticism is a good example. In the Stalin era the press was full of self-criticism in the form of articles attacking maladministration and abuse. The targets of criticism, as well as the style and tactics, were chosen at the center in accord with an overall plan of political agitation. Stalin himself probably made many of the decisions. Many current complaints are still in line with a general program. But now they give the impression of far greater spontaneity, as if little people were really letting off steam about local grievances that reflect structural failures in the Soviet system.

Rather than elaborate on this theme any further I will proceed at once to the main danger. It is this: as the old controls are slackened, popular demands on the regime are practically certain to rise. De Tocqueville in a famous passage on the beginnings of the French Revolution caught the essence of this process: "The evil suffered patiently as inevitable seems unendurable as soon as one conceives the idea of escaping from it. All of the abuses that have been removed seem only to delineate better those that remain and to make one's feelings more bitter. The evil, it is true, has become less, but one's sensibility is more acute."[13] To be more specific, if consumer demands do not find more satisfaction *and* do lead to noticeable public disorder, then Gorbachev may have to give way to a "strong man" (or himself become such a figure) in order to effect some version of neo-Stalinist policies.

Neither socialist democracy nor a new socialist dictator, however, seems to be the most probable outcome. It is rather more likely that after much sound and quite a bit of fury there will be little real reform. At some point down this road a leader could proclaim the victory of *perestroika* and argue that there is no need for any more of it. Or he could just let the campaign die out and drop the expression down the memory hole. Then the old system could continue lurching and limping along with a bit of new public-relations decoration.

That outcome would be a tragedy, not only for Gorbachev but for the rest of the world too. Gorbachev begins to look like a leader of the last cavalry charge of humane yet secular rationalism in a world dominated by anti-rationalism and chauvinist religious fundamentalism. Perhaps he will turn out to be the last flare-up from the ashes of the Enlightenment. But if the flame goes out, how many people are there now who would notice the difference?

By late 1997 the prospects for an effective liberal regime had hardly become more encouraging. To be sure there are positive changes since Stalinist times. Russian leaders no longer resolve major political issues by shooting or jailing opponents. From time to time there also appear signs of a lively intellectual life including opposition to the authorities of the day. However, this encouraging aspect seems precarious. In the cultural sphere there is also a negative trend, noticeable too in other former Leninist societies: a passionate thirst among young elites for the most stultifying hedonism so prominent in Western popular culture. Thus these supposedly liberal features, on inspection, begin to look like symptoms of fragility rather than incipient democratic growth. Instead of autocratic decisions, the new "veto" democracy legitimates a regime of no decisions—or perhaps just enough decisions with sufficient rhetoric to gull the World Bank. This form of political paralysis is by no means confined to Russia. But there it produces widespread suffering. Large segments of the population find themselves caught

[13]Alexis de Tocqueville, *L'Ancien Régime et la Révolution* (Paris, 1952), 223.

with the worst features of both worlds, capitalist and socialist. They have lost the rudimentary social supports of socialism. In return they have gotten inflation, arrears of wages and salaries whose purchasing power may be pathetic, and substantial unemployment. Sheer despair and the absence of any persuasive alternative could prevent the situation from becoming explosive.

Social Sources of Anti-Social Behavior

What is anti-social behavior?

Leninists and fascists have no difficulty in answering this question. For them any kind of behavior apparently opposed to their regime is necessarily anti-social. So is lack of enthusiasm when the regime demands enthusiastic support. Even the suspicion that someone harbors thoughts critical of the regime, or just some of its current policies, is enough to label that person anti-social.

For liberals and democrats, however, the definition of anti-social presents some problems. A good many liberals are inclined to shy away from the expression because it seems to carry elitist and ethnocentric overtones. From this standpoint, for example, black urban riots are not anti-social because the riots at least indirectly improve the situation of many blacks by extorting concessions from whites. I agree with this interpretation. (White behavior is probably anti-social in this case.) Nevertheless there are forms of behavior that damage society without corresponding social and political gains, or with only small gains compared with the harm done.

Some examples taken from ordinary daily experience in the United States will elucidate the meaning of anti-social more effectively than vigorous wrestling with concepts and definitions. The most familiar example of anti-social behavior is that of the drunken driver who flees from the scene of an accident. Less familiar but probably more common is the fast boater (usually a male showing off) who speeds through a quiet anchorage endangering small boats with his wake and upsetting pots, pans, and crockery in larger vessels. Admonitions to slow down in accord with the law will usually generate obscenities, unless the admonition comes from a rare harbor police officer.

In this case and others the individuals who behave in an anti-social manner are likely to defend their acts by claiming a right to use or enjoy their property in ways of their own choice. Thus many middle-class Americans claim the right to let their dogs dispose of their droppings anyplace except on their own property. Animal rights are of course quite popular today, usually to the disadvantage of human medical rights. Then there is the familiar right to let the television set blare at full volume through the warm summer night when all windows are open. One might prefer to label such behavior as merely inconsiderate. But if inconsiderate behavior becomes commonplace, it is anti-social in its very frequency.

With the exception of the drunken driver, the anti-social behavior just mentioned does not as a rule have lethal consequences. Nevertheless lethal consequences are probably more widespread than we realize. Take the case of a Maine jury that in the summer of 1990 refused to convict a deer hunter who had accidentally shot and killed a woman in her own yard. The refusal to convict serves clear notice that, in Maine, society will *not* protect the innocent victims of hordes of trigger-happy hunters who swarm all over private property, even when posted with "No hunting" signs. The most serious forms of anti-social behavior, in the sense of being dangerous to large numbers of people, probably still occur in industry despite all the legislation and administrative regulation that has grown up since the turn of the century. (There was, in fact, some retraction of regulation during the Reagan years, and future prospects are far from clear.) Either the industrial product is dangerous or the plant that makes the product is dangerous, or both together. These forms of anti-social behavior have deservedly captured a great deal of attention in recent years. For that reason I shall not discuss them in any detail. It is enough to remind ourselves that they exist.

A common thread binds all of these examples together in a way that will serve as a working definition of anti-social behavior. (A working definition tells us what to look for in the course of further investigation. It blocks off a section of social reality as deserving special attention from the standpoint of a specific inquiry.) Thus anti-social behavior is the failure to carry out implicit or explicit social obligations, a failure that has consequences harmful or very disagreeable to other people. The driver who gets behind the wheel of a car while under the influence of alcohol violates the obligation to drive without being a menace to others on the road. Often the obligation itself receives no more than weak and ambiguous support from the general public or law enforcement agencies. There have been complaints about this weak enforcement in connection with drunken driving. The case of the Maine jury that refused to convict a deer hunter is much more striking. In that case there is an explicit denial of any obligation on the part of the hunter to behave responsibly and avoid killing innocent bystanders. Instead there was some attempt to put responsibility on the victim for wearing white clothing that resembled or suggested a deer in motion. The absence of weak public support for the obligation is a crucial aspect of the problem.

The burden of these observations is that any account of anti-social behavior will have to explain not only the causes behind the violation or rejection of social obligations by specific individuals and groups but also analyze the degree of support or lack of it behind the obligation itself. An increase in anti-social behavior can arise from the deterioration and increasing ambiguity of old obligations as well as the failure to create new ones. Industrial growth in an ever more crowded planet has already led to the demand for new social obligations to protect our environment, a demand that has by no means earned universal support. Finally any inquiry into anti-social behavior has to remember the message of the *Antigone*. Obligations with powerful emotional charges can conflict with one another. What looks like piety and concern for the general welfare from one point of view appears as blasphemy and capricious tyranny from another.

At this point the whole topic of anti-social behavior may begin to appear confusing. There are just too many questions to ask. In the end confusion may well remain. There are few if any issues in the study of human affairs that have found a widely satisfactory resolution if the issues present both an intellectual and an emotional challenge. Nevertheless it may be possible to reduce the confusion considerably by classifying the main forms of social obligation in modern societies and noting how the obligations relate to anti-social behavior. We will start with obligations to authority in (1) the political arena and continue, with a steadily diminishing emphasis on authority, through (2) the arena of the economy, (3) that of sex, marriage, and the family, and finally (4) that of relations to strangers. There is no pretense of completeness in this little scheme. Rather it is a rough and ready scaffold enabling us to climb up a bit and discover what there is to see from a higher but by no means lofty vantage point.

I

The first obligation on citizens of a modern "civilized" state is to govern and be governed. Obviously the obligation to govern rests upon a small minority, while the obligation to accept their rule rests upon a large majority. The precise nature of the specific obligations inherent in ruling and being ruled also varies a great deal between authoritarian political systems and more democratic ones. Yet there is one common feature: the obligation to maintain domestic peace and order—most of the time. There is also another specific obligation: the military and patriotic one to oppose the enemies of the state by service in the armed forces. There is wide variation on this score as well. At one end of the spectrum we find the military obligations of a large predatory state such as Nazi Germany. At the other end of the spectrum there is the strictly defensive apparatus of a small state such as Switzerland.

The refusal on a wide scale to meet these two obligations leads to the disintegration of political authority and hence of the state itself. In the case of the Nazis one can claim that such refusal was really a pro-social act rather than an anti-social one. But under that kind of tyranny, refusal and resistance were almost impossible. What resistance did exist was quite ineffective. Such a polity prohibits the most important kind of opposition, one that would make major changes in the system of rule, and thus the most important kind of pro-social behavior.

In less tyrannical states political disintegration sets in when the central authority loses legitimacy because it cannot satisfy the often sharply conflicting demands of different segments of the population. Intransigeance in making these demands has anti-social consequences even if the demands are justified on other grounds. An oppressed minority can make life worse for itself, and much worse for the majority, if its demands make a generally tolerable society ungovernable. (The decision of the German Communists to oppose the Weimar Republic comes to mind in this connection.) Financial difficulties, especially in the form of sharp disputes over the burden of taxes, are another symptom of deteriorating authority. In these cases self-interest easily takes priority over the general welfare in an anti-social manner. Nowadays it is hard to locate any concern for the general welfare in the ebb and flow of political discussion in the United States. War, perhaps the most expensive luxury of "civilization," has often intensified the strain on legitimacy and group conflict after a brief period of initial euphoria. If the context intensifies, it reaches a stage when the central authority can no longer count on obedience. There is a paralysis of order, as in the final stages of the Weimar Republic or the end of the monarchy in the French Revolution.

The state may then break up into a series of groups trying to establish their authority by force, often in a restricted territory. By this point the society's connective tissue has dissolved. The society breaks up into its constituent parts or interest groups. Of these the most vociferous nowadays are liable to be religious and ethnic minorities. Even before the point of dissolution everybody has rights. Nobody has obligations. By 1991 it was obvious that the USSR was moving rapidly in this direction. In the United States similar lines of fracture have been apparent for some years.

When and if such trends approach their extreme limits, personal security almost disappears due to the impossibility of maintaining order. Likewise the use of force, revolutionary or popular-reactionary, to restore order and maintain territorial integrity will almost certainly claim numerous victims.

The next obligation on citizens of a modern state is to work. It is second mainly from the standpoint of convenience in exposition, though one can argue that without peace and order created by the political realm the economic realm can scarcely function. Work means taking part in the production of goods and services and also in social arrangements for the distribution of these goods. Work also includes rules about honesty in the quality of the goods and services as well as in the practices of distribution and exchange. The obligations inherent in these rules of honest working behavior are subject to widespread evasion.

There is nothing fundamentally new about these evasions. They flourished for instance in religion-soaked medieval London, which demonstrates that such evasions are not the product of the decline of morality under advanced capitalism. Instead evasions are likely to appear wherever exchanges become important and replace production by the household for its own use.

In general the economy appears to be that part of a modern social system where the sense of moral obligation is weakest. There the whole notion of obligation is cloudy and subject to conflicting obligations. Dishonesty appears to be rife wherever it is not plainly visible to the potential victim. But this image may be exaggerated because dishonesty makes interesting news, which honesty seldom does. No deal or business arrangement is possible, after all, unless one can trust a prior verbal agreement to do thus and so. Nor will a strictly worded contract, drawn up after a verbal agreement, be of much use in holding a dishonest person to his word.

On occasion one hears the claim that the central commandment of American business morality is to get as rich as possible as fast as possible by any means that succeed without getting caught. Were that really the case on a wide scale, all social obligations would dissolve. Nobody would have to do anything for anybody: spouse, children, employees, business associates, or government officials. The successful plutocrat, male or fe-male, would be a caricature of the Nietzschean hero, above and beyond good and evil. But the plutocrat could only preside briefly over a society disintegrated into chaos and anarchy. There have been tendencies in this direction during the Age of the Robber Barons. It is by no means clear that these tendencies have disappeared with the rise of the more imper-sonal giant corporation. Yet it is quite plain that this particular form of amoral and anti-social behavior does not dominate the American social scenery. There must be powerful obstacles in its way and powerful social forces arrayed against it.

I doubt that the preaching of the preachers, the plaints of the intellec-tuals, the proliferation of courses on ethics in business schools and un-dergraduate curricula, contribute much to the effective opposition. Vicious self-interest can break through such obstacles like a cannon ball through a cobweb. The obstacle may lie in quite a different area. It is extraordinarily difficult to act in a completely amoral and anti-social man-ner, doing so with ever increasing success. Such behavior requires contin-ual alertness, quick and accurate judgment. It is much easier to act in accord with general social expectations. Furthermore, the more villainous one's behavior the more necessary it is to maintain a visible front of be-nign amiability and good character. Otherwise there is a risk of disrepute and even jail. To sum up, the risk of this particular form of potentially dangerous anti-social behavior does seem to be a self-limiting one.

In addition to plain and fancy dishonesty there are a number of other forms of economic behavior that at one time or another have been widely regarded as anti-social. They include monopolies, tariffs, smuggling, trade unions, and black markets. The reason for regarding these arrangements as anti-social is because they divert resources "unjustly" from one set of people to another set. The arrangements are "unjust," evidently, to the extent that they produce distributive results different from those that would occur under a free competitive market. In other words only such a free market produces a morally acceptable distribution, a judgment that has never commanded universal assent. Black markets put in an appear-ance only under a command economy where goods and services are ra-tioned according to political and ethical criteria. Under a free competitive economy where goods and services exchange in accord with market prices a black market cannot exist. When a black market comes into existence, it withdraws goods and services from politically and ethically determined purposes. Let us assume that these purposes are widely recognized as legitimate. Then this withdrawal of goods and services from the legitimate economic arena works only to the advantage of those who can patronize the black market because they are rich enough or have the right connections or both. In that case there is a net loss to the social order. Hence one can consider the black market as anti-social under these conditions.

But, as anyone familiar with the workings of socialist economies knows, that is not the only possibility. Frequent shortages and bottlenecks plague socialist industry. A socialist plant may be threatened with a prolonged shutdown if management cannot locate quickly a scarce part or a rare chemical essential to a complex manufacturing process. The usual procedure in such cases is to locate the missing part or ingredient through semilegal or illegal channels — in other words a black market. In this case the resort to a black market is necessary to keep the wheels of industry turning.

An illegal and presumably anti-social arrangement turns out to play an indispensable role in the workings of the whole society. This is a splendid illustration of the ambiguity of human social arrangements and a warning against premature and oversimplified assessments of these arrangements.

The third set of obligations we have to consider is the series connected with sex, marriage, and the family. Though elements of inequality certainly remain, these obligations are more among equals, especially in modern times, than is the case with political and economic institutions.

In western theory and practice from biblical times onward there has been a powerful attempt to channel the sexual drive into the service of procreation pure and simple. One fairly obvious reason for limiting sexual partners and pleasures has been the desire to keep clear the line of descent for property, that is to avoid suspicions about the fatherhood of the youngster who will inherit the family property. With high death rates there is also a strong social concern about continuing to renew the population.

Yet these explanations hardly seem adequate to account for the ferocity against all forms of nonprocreative sexuality. Two other explanations may clarify such ferocity. First of all in many individuals the sexual drive *is* so powerful as to be terrifying. It seems a power outside the individual. Whether the drive is more powerful in females or males has been an issue about which opposite opinions (nearly always male opinions) have prevailed during different epochs of western history. In turn the drive needs, or seems to need terrifying sanctions to control it. Second, sexual attachments and sexual pleasures are earthly pleasures, and, at least for a time, very intense pleasures. Hence they distract attention and energy from other affairs. That is especially true of religious affairs in a religion of salvation. If this life on earth can present such joys, why should there be such a fuss about the life to come?[1]

The picture of a continuous and frequently frantic effort to channel the sexual drive into "legitimate" and purely reproductive acts does need a bit of shading and qualification. In classical antiquity there was an important relaxation of these controls in the form of Athenian toleration for homosexual attachments between an adolescent boy and a mature man. The relationship was tolerated rather than approved. If it lasted too long, and especially if the older man continued too long with such pleasure, the result was severe social disapproval. Likewise it seems probable, though by no means certain, that in Christian times ecclesiastical and secular forms of the prevailing *Sittenpolizei* were seldom able to impose strict standards on the very top or the very bottom of the social hierarchy. Finally in the early days of Christianity there was a movement against procreation in the form of asceticism that tried to banish sex altogether from human life. On the other hand, to my limited knowledge the abolition or suppression of sexual drives was never more than an ideal for those who felt capable of pursuing it. Abstinence was not for everybody.

Against this background we can now see clearly what anti-social behavior has meant for a long time in western societies. The only form of socially approved sexual behavior—and on occasion even this approval was grudging—has been intercourse in marriage for the purpose of having children. Everything else was prohibited and regarded as anti-social. (The term "anti-social" has not been used. Instead the behavior has been condemned as "evil," "against religion," "against nature" or "unnatural." The relatively weak "immoral" seems to have come into usage rather late.) The forms of prohibited or anti-social behavior were adultery, homosexuality, lesbianism, anal sex, oral sex, and masturbation.[2] Penalties for these acts varied in severity, in some cases including the death penalty, generally by burning. However, since there does not appear to have been any overall agreement on the penalties, there is nothing to be gained by examining this aspect further. One point, however, does deserve mention: lesbian behavior was almost socially invisible.[3]

---

[1]This joy and abandonment is quite apparent in Abelard's letters. Hence his abandonment of Heloise to the tune of lofty moral lectures impresses a modern reader as obnoxious irresponsibility. See *The Letters of Abelard and Heloise*, translated with an introduction by Betty Radice (New York, 1974).

[2]Both Webster's *Ninth New Collegiate Dictionary* (1983) and *The Oxford Universal Dictionary on Historical Principles* (3d ed. revised, 1955) give the year 1660 for the first known use of the word "immoral."

[3]Judith C. Brown, *Immodest Acts: The Life of a Lesbian Nun in Renaissance Italy* (New

These prohibitions lasted with little erosion right through the nineteenth century and beyond, until after the middle of the twentieth century. Then in the 1960s they disappeared, at least in wide sectors of the articulate middle class, as if an avalanche hovering on the cliffs of a mountain had been loosened by the spring sun and crashed down to bury everything in its wake. The reasons for this sudden destruction of traditional sexual morality are not easy to determine. One may have been the discovery of contraceptive devices for women that were easy to use and seemed harmless. Another may have been the general rejection of authority by the young that the war in Vietnam produced, or precipitated if one believes that it occurred when it did due to other deeper causes. This golden age of the sexual revolution lasted only for about twenty years, at which point AIDS, or Jehovah's revenge, arose. Just what effect AIDS may have is uncertain. Many youngsters and people not so young display the attitude that disaster cannot strike me. Nevertheless AIDS will certainly impose some restraints on casual hedonism. But they will be self-imposed prudential restraints, not obedience to quasi-divine rules and superior moral authority.

This situation leaves us with the question of what kinds of sexual behavior, if any, may on objective grounds still be regarded as anti-social under present day conditions? The obvious candidate is promiscuity. Quite aside from its medical consequences promiscuity is potentially more damaging than the traditional sexual evils of adultery and so forth, or else includes one or more of these as a special form of promiscuity. If asceticism is anti-social because it imposes excessive restraint, promiscuity might be viewed as anti-social because it is the result of an undue lack of restraint.

However, it is hard to give an objective and unambiguous definition of promiscuity. How many different partners must a person have in order to be considered promiscuous? Putting down a specific number would just be funny. Likewise, how often must a change of partners take place? Obviously most of the answers come from that protean entity so dear to some contemporary lawyers: prevailing community standards. Still, one might be able to go a step further and risk a definition based on apparent anti-social consequences.

By this reasoning one might consider promiscuity to be a change of sexual partners so frequent as to rule out the possibility of a couple raising their own children. But why do we have to impose the obligation of

York, 1986), 9, 17. Chapter 1 of this book provides a useful survey of official medieval attitudes toward sexual deviance.

raising children on everybody, especially when there are good reasons for regarding even the rich countries as overpopulated? Married couples are no longer subject to criticism if they do not or can not have children. If everybody decided to avoid the obligation of having children and just flitted from one partner to another in search of the latest pleasures, the consequences would of course be lethal for the human society. Since that situation is hardly the case, the threat to marriage—or equivalents to marriage—does not provide adequate grounds for treating promiscuity as anti-social.

There is, I suggest, a much stronger basis for this critical judgment. Promiscuous behavior sooner or later involves the neglect or outright rejection of responsibility for and obligations to a sexual partner. This rejection of responsibility is, I believe, the essential feature of promiscuity and belongs in any definition thereof. The responsibility is both material and emotional. At the very least each partner has an obligation to keep the household going with food and shelter, to cherish and support the other partner in sickness as well as health, stormy times as well as sunny ones. If all this sounds much like marriage, it should sound that way. Marriage is the social recognition of a couple's mutual obligations. Males are probably the most guilty of neglecting these obligations. Many a male expects his female partner to produce a gourmet dinner and an intriguing sexual experience without having to make any returns himself. Clearly such behavior is both exploitative and anti-social. It is the woman who pays the freight in terms of lowered esteem and perhaps reduced earning power. For this and other reasons younger women—and some men— have observed that it must have been men who put across the sexual revolution of the 1960s because men were the only real winners from the change. For many women sexual liberation turned out to be serial bondage to male caprice.

The rejection of obligations to a sexual partner is the most obviously anti-social form of sexual behavior. This is an obligation for the most part among equals, at least in contemporary western society. It is a horizontal obligation in contrast to vertical obligations that are perceived to possess a more legitimate form of authority. Now we may look a little further at horizontal obligations by examining obligations to and among strangers.

The United States is historically and sociologically a long way from ancient Greece where the stranger had an element of divinity and could expect to be both protected and received as an honored guest. Nevertheless even now the stranger here still enjoys strongly enforced rights of protection in the sense that there is an obligation to rescue a person who falls into danger even when such a person or persons is quite unknown to the rescuers. The plainest illustration of the obligation to rescue occurs in the case of a mishap or more serious accident at sea or in the mountains. There is a certain camaraderie among sailors and mountaineers because both the sea and the mountains can at times be dangerous, often enough with little warning, or a warning whose threat is apparent only to someone with extended experience. The obligation to attempt a rescue at sea has a legal sanction as well as a moral one. I am not aware of a legal one in the case of a mountaineering accident. But the moral obligation to try for a rescue, even at the risk of one's own life, is equally strong. Anyone who fails to attempt a rescue where the need is obvious is subject to the most severe criticism. Anyone with a special license, such as mountain guide or master mariner, would lose the license for deliberate refusal to attempt a rescue where one was feasible. Actually such refusals are extremely rare. Conformity to expected behavior occurs not because the sanctions for failure are so strong but because the demand to render help has such force behind it.

Even without the camaraderie that comes from shared danger there can be an obligation to rescue. Familiar examples are attempts to rescue someone who has fallen through the ice, a child who has tumbled into a well or some other dangerous spot. Our "common humanity" acquires concrete meaning in the case of danger to one or a few persons. But not always. If there are numerous bystanders and witnesses to the accident, the responsibility for action may not fall clearly on any one individual. Then there is liable to be a period of confusion before the rescue starts.

In all these cases there is likely to be some inclination to call in the specialists to take over responsibility: the fire department, the police department, the coast guard, a rescue team of mountain guides, or in winter, the avalanche specialist. When it succeeds, this move relieves the ordinary bystander of any obligation to help. Presumably the specialists can do the job better. But only too often they cannot. They may be too far away to bring help in time. And even if they do come, they may, unfortunately, be grossly incompetent. Hence it is unlikely that the ordinary citizen can shed this obligation altogether.

Do ordinary citizens want to shed this burden? Probably there is a wide range of feelings about the obligation to help a stranger in crisis. There is such a thing as pity and identification with the victim. There is also the hope of acclaim for executing an heroic rescue. Alternatively there may be acute risk in any attempt to render assistance. In between, yet very important, are considerations about the expenditure of time, energy, and resources on behalf of an unknown stranger. These considerations help us to understand the tragic fate of Kitty Genovese. On 13 March 1964 this young woman was stabbed to death on the street in a middle-class section of Queens amid unheeded cries for help. Later the police located thirty-eight people who watched the murder for about half an hour from the windows of their apartments. Only one called the police, but only after getting advice on what to do by first telephoning a friend. By then it was too late. Kitty was dead. Questioned by the police later about their refusal to intervene some witnesses said they did not want to get involved. Others said they were tired. (It was about 3:30 in the morning.) At least one or two others thought the whole episode was a lovers' quarrel. All of them in effect claimed that it was none of their business. More accurately, they did not want this murder to be any of their business.[4]

In a big city middle-class individuals have to perceive acute human suffering and define it as none of their business if they are to continue earning their living and behaving in an otherwise "normal" fashion. The thirty-eight witnesses' behavior was a pathological extension of this normal behavior. Another reason why Kitty Genovese's cries for help found no answer is that she had no friends who could help in the apartment building where she lived. That is the usual structure of friendship in a city. Friendships arise at work and elsewhere, and friends may live all over the city. But one may not even know the telephone number of the person next door. (Although in really poor sections this is less true.) To sum up, this tragedy was the result of urban social organization and urban mentality. If a similar attack had occurred in a small rural community where everyone knew everybody else—even if they often hated each other—the result would have been very different.

The practice of calling upon society's specialized and professional services has become almost universal in the case of a much more numerous group of strangers, those in economic distress. A person who finds it impossible to make a living, and has no resources on which to fall back, either goes on welfare or is put on welfare. The process of becoming a welfare recipient, often a rather complicated bureaucratic affair, generally takes place out of sight of those who must accept the obligation of supporting welfare through taxes. This is not an obligation the ordinary cit-

[4] A. M. Rosenthal, *Thirty-Eight Witnesses* (New York, 1964). The author was metropolitan editor of the *New York Times* when this event occurred and supervised the paper's coverage of it. For an attempt to explain the witnesses' failure to act, see also Stanley Milgram and Paul Hollander, "The Murder They Heard," *The Nation*, 15 June 1964.

izen can accept or refuse. In fact the ordinary individual taxpayer has only a limited input into the level of taxes he or she must pay. Because taxes are mandatory and the benefits, if any, that they create through the welfare system are largely invisible, this particular social obligation creates a great deal of resentment. (Since taxes are hard to escape, particularly local taxes for such purposes, there is little evasion of this obligation.) This resentment takes the form of complaints about "welfare cheats" and about the creation of a large number of people who have become so dependent on welfare that they cannot or will not hold a job. These criticisms are by no means completely without foundation. To assess them here is neither possible nor necessary. For our purposes the significant point in these criticisms is their effort to claim that it is the welfare system itself that has anti-social consequences. From this standpoint "our common humanity" ceases to exist at the door of the tax collector's office. Along with other currents of opinion these criticisms have led to a sharp reduction in funds for welfare. If these trends continue, there may be a serious political clash between the haves and have nots and a new surge of crime and personal tragedies among those living close to the margin. There is after all, not a great deal of living space left along the subway tracks. But welfare is not a real solution to the problem of unintentional poverty. There is a limit to the number of people on welfare that any society can tolerate and still produce enough to go around.

II

Having seen the variety of forms anti-social behavior may take, we are now ready to move toward an explanation. First let us look again at what anti-social behavior amounts to. Anti-social behavior is the rejection of obligations not only to figures of authority but also to equals and fellow members of society. It is a refusal of allegiance, obedience, and civic obligations in the area of politics. It is a rejection of the obligation to work and a refusal to join any form of social coordination with an element of command in the economic arena. It generalizes a refusal of responsibility to others in connection with sex, marriage, and the family. It fosters a relationship to neighbors, friends, and strangers in which they appear only as possible sources of gratification, not as persons whom one has an obligation to assist in cases of danger and distress.

From this little summary it is obvious that human society would disintegrate in any part of the world where this became the predominant pattern of behavior. It is also obvious that this little summary is a caricature of that familiar figure, economic man. Since we all know reasonably well how economic man came into existence, we have taken a large step in the direction of the explanation we have been seeking. Before we try to decide where that step leads us, however, it will be wise to make some factual observations to put this caricature in perspective.

First of all selfishness and a reluctance to carry out a social obligation are not unique products of contemporary civilization. One is likely to find this behavior in any society, including the cooperative non-literate semiutopias so appealing to modern romantics. Remember the Tikopian who stole fish for his private consumption from the nets used in the collective catch. Neither angels nor socialists, human beings are not well designed for living in society, without which, on the other hand, they would all rapidly die. A good deal of friction, evasion, and quarreling is inevitable even under the most favorable conditions.

Second, in periods of sustained structural change, such as that in Western society since the Middle Ages, old loyalties continually become obsolete as new ones take their place. There is nothing pathological in other words about the decay of "traditional" obligations. The problem lies in what replaces them, because society without obligation is impossible. We cannot have all rights and no duties. Here indeed is a major focus of concern about modern civilization. It is hard to discern any new system of obligations to replace those presently displaying serious signs of decay. There was a time not so long ago when socialism was expected to be the new ethical replacement for a moribund capitalism. No one can take that hope seriously any longer, even if fears for capitalism may turn out to be justified. An even more serious cause for worry is that none of the current contenders for a moral-social supremacy can speak in terms of pan-human concerns. They are all ethnic or nationalist doctrines, or else some form of religious fundamentalism.

Finally it is by no means altogether clear that social and moral disintegration is worse in our own time than it has been at some points in the past. Consider the big city as the center of decay. If one reads the *New York Times* for a couple of weeks focusing on the local news, one can easily come away with the sense that the situation is hopeless. The authorities cannot possibly cope with the "inner barbarians" or do anything about the social causes that produce them. But was not the threat to life and property just as great in eighteenth-century London?[5]

[5] M. Dorothy George, *London Life in the Eighteenth Century* (1925; Harmondsworth, 1966), intro., chaps. 1 and 6.

With these warnings against overemphasizing both the novelty and the intensity of our present evils, we may return to the problem of accounting for them in the form of economic man. If such a person ever could exist, it would be someone almost without social obligations and certainly without loyalties. The only obligations would be fleeting and changing social relationships entered into strictly on grounds of probable personal advantage. To repeat, this is a caricature. But it is a caricature of quite recognizable social trends. Stendahl's Julien Sorel and Budd Schulberg's Sammy Glick are two familiar fictional examples created roughly a century apart. At a more general level, and perhaps as a reaction against the "really existing economic man" manifested in the continental bourgeoisie of the late nineteenth century, the completely amoral hero, the individual *moribus solutus* became a favorite literary figure. Gide's early novels contain striking examples. More recently Alberto Moravia's novels treat women forced in that direction. It is highly likely that these fictional themes reflect wishes, hopes, *and* fears among their actual and potential readers.

Two related yet distinct trends that long antedate modern industrialism, while becoming an important part of it, go a long way toward explaining this erosion of social obligations. One is the demand for social equality that struck Tocqueville so forcibly when industrial society was still well over the historical horizon. It is hard to accept an obligation to someone when you are convinced that you are every bit as good as that person. The other trend passes under the name of secular rationalism. For our purposes its main effect was to demystify traditional forms of authority, both secular and religious. The corrosive effects of the market on older social relationships intensified these trends. In all these ways the sense of obligation to social superiors deteriorated.

None of these trends seem to have had any overpowering effect on horizontal obligations, those to neighbors and strangers. It is unlikely, however, that horizontal obligations can become the ground for a more general restoration of the sense of obligation. That has to come about in connection with a specific social function. In the workplace, for example, one has work to acceptable standards of quality—i.e., that faucets don't leak when they are supposed to be fixed, and that one does not quit the job until it is done. "Love thy neighbor," is not a useful injunction for that purpose. We need a sense of duty and pride in workmanship.

The intellectual current of secular rationalism has by now pretty much run out into the sand. Indeed a good many influential thinkers regard secular rationalism as the cause of our major ailments from big bureaucracy to big bombs. With the blunting of the rational thrust all the traditional nonsense of the past comes to the surface along with new forms.

Intellectual battles that appeared to be finished more than fifty years ago now have to be fought over again, very likely with more tired troops and fewer ones on the side of intelligence and decency. In this area, too, the opponents of "cold" rationality want to place some form of generalized and "warm" human love as the basis for their emotional, intellectual, and social constructions. I doubt very much that any workable set of social obligations can be constructed in this manner. These romantics are almost certainly correct in claiming that no human society or even a small part of one can be built on a basis of strict rationality. In order to work together human beings apparently need at the very least a good dose of emotion to keep the friction down. Yet no good is likely to come out of building obligations mainly out of love. The units that come out of such a process are liable to be too small. For this reason and others they would probably be at each other's throats in short order. Groups whose members ostensibly love one another, such as small revolutionary groups, religious groups, governments in exile, ethnic political movements, often display vicious hostility to competing outsiders, as well as equally savage factionalism on the inside. There is enough of this in the world already without trying to make more under the banner of love versus "inhuman" rationality.

III

Is there then anything at all one can do about anti-social behavior? Can a social science informed by an historical perspective suggest any remedy?

The answer depends heavily on the brand or brands of social sciences upon which one draws and, more specifically, on the kinds of causes one perceives through that particular intellectual lens. For instance a behaviorist would probably be quite sanguine about changing anti-social behavior. From this standpoint changing anti-social behavior is no more difficult than changing any other kind of behavior. All one has to do is set up the proper system of rewards for desired behavior and penalties for undesired behavior and the hoped for results will soon be evident. However, behaviorists are liable to run into trouble when they attempt to set up their system of rewards and penalties in the context of modern American society, or any other with its existing system of social classes, distribution of political power, interest groups and so forth, instead of in a laboratory where the experimenter controls the important variables.

The behaviorists' difficulties lead us toward the other major type of explanation, one based on long-term structural and moral changes in the social order. To abbreviate greatly, this explanation sees the combination of modernization, industrialism, and secularization pushing Western society toward the dissolution of obligations and the creation of an essentially asocial economic man.[6] In and by itself no historical explanation is likely to yield a remedy because one would have to run the tape of history on a "fast rewind with erase" in order to get rid of the causes. As is well known, Marx tried to get around this difficulty by building into his account an inevitable revolutionary explosion that would enable a fresh start. Conceivably one could still write history with the aim of showing that the causes of evil and misery were weaker than commonly thought and historically limited. But doing that means demonstrating that much of one's subject matter is ephemeral, a strategy unlikely to appeal to any serious historian.

With these obstacles in mind, in casting about for a remedy I shall try for an intermediate position between the omnipotence of behaviorism and the impotence of an extreme historicism. After all in reality, some people propel historical trends while others oppose them. It is this struggle in which we are really interested.

The first step is to recognize — and get others to recognize — anti-social behavior for what it is: a serious threat to civilized existence. That is not easy. Even a mild admonition is liable to elicit a "Mind your own goddamned business!" If the encounter lasts a bit longer there is likely to be a pyrotechnic display about this being a free country where the individual has Rights. Here "rights" means that the individual can do as he pleases no matter what happens to anybody else. The person who recognizes anti-social behavior and speaks up about it has to have just a hint of iron in the soul. It is no role for the person who seeks to be agreeable and keep peace in the neighborhood even to the point of letting ethnic slurs pass in silence.

From the critical actions of a few individuals it is a short step to the formation of a loosely organized movement or pressure group. The purpose and effect of such a movement is to change the cultural assumptions and intellectual atmosphere surrounding a particular form of behavior from positive or neutral to negative and condemnatory. There have been a great many such movements in the United States, and in recent times

---

[6]The best recent statement of this view known to me is Alan Wolfe, *Whose Keeper? Social Science and Moral Obligation* (Berkeley, Calif., 1989). However, the diagnosis strikes me as far better than the remedy, a revival of community at the local level.

they have had notable successes. They range in content from civil rights movements to environmental ones, including those directed at smoking. In the case of anti-social behavior a movement probably would have to choose a specific form of anti-social behavior as its target rather than anti-social behavior in all its forms. In that sense some movements, like those against industrial dangers, already exist.

By no means are all movements socially desirable. (The Ku Klux Klan is a case in point.) The desirable ones mentioned in the preceding paragraph have by no means brought about fundamental changes in American culture and society. But they have produced some changes. That is all one can sensibly hope for. The only alternative to action based on modest hopes is to do nothing—to sit on one's hands and complain without thinking. That is merely an uncomfortable road to perdition.

Principles of Social Inequality

Equality has been a pervasive though not universal demand in human societies. Inequality has been a universal fact of human societies with a written language, as well as a fact of several nonliterate societies. In the hope of shedding light on the apparent paradox I shall review here the main principles that have governed and continue to govern inequality in human societies. Much writing on this topic has taken the form of pleas and arguments on behalf of equality combined with attacks on some form of inequality. This essay instead represents a sustained effort to explain what exists and what has existed. Here "principles" refers to the varied criteria according to which human societies judge people to be unequal and the reasons why such criteria exist and change. We shall be looking for causes and results rather than ethical justifications for inequality or ethical attacks on it.

The forms of inequality discussed here have little or nothing to do with individual qualities such as bravery in a warrior, skill in the hunter, sexual attractiveness in the young girl, and similar instances. By themselves whatever advantages such distinctions confer on an individual usually disappear with the death of that individual, even though these distinctions may be significant for the group during that person's lifetime. Such distinctions are not institutionalized and passed along to the next generation. They are not as such the basis of a system of social classes, though the upper classes usually claim to possess more socially desirable qualities than the lower classes. Our interest here is in institutionally created and supported forms of inequality.

II

We may begin the concrete analysis of inequality with a brief discussion of two principles, age and sex. To the best of my limited knowledge every known human society draws distinctions along these two axes. Their universality distinguishes them from the sources of inequality in the more complex societies, sometimes also referred to as high cultures, to be discussed shortly. In these latter cultures inequality arises from internally generated social causes usually mingled with elements of force and fraud derived from such things as a history of conquest.

There is a wide range of variation in the nature and meaning of social distinctions according to age and sex. Among highly mobile peoples living close to the margin of existence, old people may not be able to keep up on a day's march. Among such people there is the custom of killing the old. Our own society belongs near the opposite end of the spectrum. Demographically we produce more and more old people, and devote more and more resources to taking care of them. That happens because the old are fairly well organized politically. Even our society's greater resources do not provide enough humane care, as defined by our society, for all old people who need it. Therefore it is an open question whether the "primitive" killing of the old causes more or less suffering than the "care" provided — and not provided — in our society.

Allocations and treatment by sex may display a somewhat smaller range of variation than those by age. Just about everywhere the tasks that require steadiness and application, without huge bursts of strength, have fallen to women. As a group they have played hardly any role in politics, though there have been a scattering of talented female rulers and a few vicious ones. Nor do women have much to display in the way of leadership and attainments in warfare, the economy, and even religions. Feminists have yet to make a persuasive contrary case. Among historians and social scientists there is not a great deal of dispute about the facts of widespread female subordination. Disagreements begin with attempts to assess the extent to which the inequalities are due to biological factors or are historically determined (and therefore subject to changing and changeable social and historical causes). This argument has been going on as long as the present writer can remember without any sign of emerging agreement. As it would be absurd to try to resolve the issue here, I shall confine myself to a few brief comments that apply especially to the contemporary situation in advanced industrial countries.

Motherhood is a special social role confined to women. It has both biological and social aspects, especially in the rearing of children. This special role continues to exist in modern societies where the advantages of superior physical strength, the source of male superiority in the past, have greatly diminished. (The advantages have by no means altogether disappeared, as one can notice from watching the work of carpenters, plumbers, mechanics, and other similar trades.) Motherhood takes a woman out of the labor force for a brief period of time before and immediately after the birth of a child. This experience adds an obligation that consumes a great deal of time and energy. Many women find the task of continuing to work while raising a child quite overwhelming. Even in economically advanced societies this special burden is liable to remain a heavy tax on female energies and capacities for an indefinite future. The burden can be somewhat reduced by a cooperative and understanding husband, and a great deal more by hiring other women, either as individual nurses, domestic servants or as the staff of collective organizations such as day care centers, to take the burden off the mother's shoulders. But hiring help means that well-to-do women put the burden of child-care on the shoulders of the less well-to-do. That is the case no matter who pays for this care. For women as a whole the burden is still there and reduces their prospects of accomplishment in all fields of endeavor. For the foreseeable future there appears to be no prospect of fundamental change in this situation.

III

Social inequalities based on age and sex crystallize around physiological inequalities. They are the main foci of inequality in simple nonliterate societies. Though these two foci continue to have effect in complex literate societies, other and more strictly social and historical causes of inequality overshadow them by far.

Civilized or complex societies (i.e., those with a written language and based initally on agriculture, the production of artisans, trade, and, as a rule, some predatory activities ranging from piracy to large scale warfare) grant very unequal rewards to the series of social activities that supply their material and spiritual requirements. As human societies evolved from pre-industrial civilizations to our present electronic-nuclear one, the number and types of these activities have greatly increased. If the nuclear age does not turn out to be the last phase of human civilization, the increase can be expected to continue. Despite this growing complexity it is possible to construct a rough and ready classification of five major types of social activities that applies to both pre-industrial agrarian societies and modern industrial ones.

The first type of social activity is governing or control over people. By that I mean primarily social coordination or seeing to it that socially necessary tasks are carried out on time and in the proper relation to each other. In my judgment social coordination is the most important and most difficult task facing human societies. Nearly any human undertaking that needs a considerable number of people to execute it requires coordination through command-obedience relationships. (We shall consider exceptions shortly.) These relationships can at times be soft and gentle and even pseudo-egalitarian, as in a large business firm where office employees may use first names in talking with the firm's officers. Nevertheless everyone in the firm knows who the bosses are. In a military or police organization, as well as some forms of ecclesiastical organizations such as the Catholic Church, the command-obedience relationships are clear, obvious, and frequently painful to subordinates. Gentleness can of course occur as well in these strictly hierarchical organizations on occasion, though it is blatantly manipulative.

The point that requires emphasis is that, outside a few small nonliterate societies, social coordination through command-obedience relationships — masked and gentle, or strict and hierarchical — is pervasive throughout human history. It is the way to get things done that have to be done in societies with a recorded history. In that sense it has a powerful rational component. In that sense too the modern romantic complaint against manipulative social behavior goes much too far. Even the simplest conversation is manipulative insofar as it is an attempt to persuade someone to think or do something.

To emphasize the rational and benign aspects of command-obedience relationships and the inequality that arises from them does not, or at least should not, imply neglect of the cruel aspects of governing. Force and fraud have certainly been major themes in human history. Organized governments may have been the worst offenders because they have had the most power to inflict danage on other people. Yet the situation has frequently been even worse whenever and wherever the formal government has broken down or been seriously weakened. Europe's Dark Ages as reported by Gregory of Tours have their parallels in both China and India during periods of weak rule.

Force and fraud are of course not identical. Still they are both ways of taking goods and services from one set of people and handing them over to someone else without adding anything to the general social product. For these reasons social inequality based on force and fraud is anything but rational and socially benign. Since so much of inequality in the course of history has been based on both force and fraud, it is hardly surprising that thoughtful people have decided we ought to dispense with rulers and inequality altogether. These neo-anarchists forget that the situation has become even worse without government, as well as the necessity for rational authority for socially benign purposes.

One cannot discuss social coordination without mentioning control over the instruments of violence—armies, navies, and, since the nineteenth century in Europe, the police—as sources and upholders of inequality. It is worth drawing attention to the fact that this is by no means an exclusively modern situation. In the Roman Empire first the praetorian guard and later the provincial armies came to dominate in the choice of emperor. On the other hand the empire had little or nothing in the way of domestic police. Only recently has there come to be scholarly interest in the far-reaching political consequences of changes in the organization of European armies during the late Middle Ages and early modern times. Brian Downing sees such changes, correctly I believe, as the major determinant of dictatorial and democratic outcomes in the twentieth century. Systematic police terror on a worldwide scale under fascism and communism is of course an achievement of twentieth-century civilization. Yet after the deaths of Hitler, Stalin, and Mao, signs appeared that this achievement was becoming historically obsolete.

The second social function is control, or perhaps attempted control, over the unexpected, the unpredictable and threatening. For millennia this was the task of the priest. Frequently but not always the priest also upheld and sanctioned public morality. That too was a way of warding off danger from the unknown. By and large, the ruler, flanked by the military and the priesthood, dominated pre-industrial societies.

Ever since the seventeenth century, scientific and secular explanations have been pressing religious ones into the background. The newer explanations and techniques may have been harder for ordinary people to understand. But they work better. Since the end of the Second World War there have been increasing signs of a reversal of this trend toward secular rationality. Natural scientists and doctors have lost some authority and prestige. Correspondingly there has been an increase in the visibility and appeal of the antirationalist forms of religion.

The fourth social function is the production and distribution of goods and services. From the standpoint of the study of inequality two aspects deserve consideration.

First, the dominant groups discussed so far—royal officials and the upper ranks of the priesthood and the military—do not engage directly in the production of food and other material goods. Instead the subordinate classes have to generate an economic surplus that the dominant classes appropriate for their own use including the creation and consumption of high culture. (The actual creation of high culture is often done by individuals from lower strata at the behest of those with high status.) The ways in which the dominant strata "pump out" a surplus, to use the Marxist expression, varies considerably over time and place. Taxes in kind and in cash along with legally required labor services constitute the central obligations. For historians and social scientists the character of the pumping out process offers a major key to understanding any specific society, especially its system of inequality. The pumping out process reveals how inequality works: who gains, who loses and why.

In the second place, within the system of production and distribution there often exist important forms of coordination without authority. Individuals make and distribute goods and services without being ordered to do so. We can distinguish two forms of nonhierarchical distribution. One is simply custom, most noticeable in nonliterate societies where it often displays egalitarian traits. The Russian mir is an instance from a literate society. Custom, however, may also be part of a hierarchical society, as in the case of the peasants' feudal dues to their overlord. The other form is the market.

In modern societies the market, where it is allowed to work freely, is a remarkable form of nonhierarchical coordination. Unlike custom it can be completely impersonal. Responding only to the cues of price, individuals can decide what to produce, how to combine labor and capital in production, how many people will receive the goods, and where. The general result of market economics on the other hand is far from egalitarian. An economist, whose name I can no longer recall, once remarked that the market faithfully reproduces all the injustices in the prevailing society. More than that, it seems that in a market society the rich do get richer and the poor get poorer. Advantages beget more advantages on one side of an exchange relationship, and the converse is also true. But the only alternative to the market in modern societies is a bureaucratic command economy, which is often much worse both economically and politically.

Fortunately in the domain of actual practice the choice is not so stark as one between a free market and a command economy. Both socialist and capitalist economies permit market prices in some sectors of the economy and the administrative controls over prices and production in other sectors. Both egalitarian-ethical ideals and other political ideals, such as a general social necessity or the security and grandeur of the state continue to serve as justifications for removing some economic activities from the control of the market. Mixed economies are subject to some internal tensions because the free market and administratively controlled areas compete with each other. Popular dissatisfaction with the workings of the market lead to demands for political control and vice versa. However, all these societies work after a fashion. In any case, no civilized society has yet come anywhere near satisfying everybody.

The pumping out of an economic surplus has obvious inegalitarian consequences even in those rare cases where the surplus serves primarily to support and create peace, order, and culture. Economic institutions without authority, such as the rare cases of factories run mainly by the workers, have at times noticeable egalitarian consequences. The case of the market is ambiguous.

Now we may turn to the division of labor, an aspect of economic production in all known societies, that is widely held to be a major source of social inequality and in all likelihood a permanent one. The division of labor reflects a society's historically created level of technology. In very simple nonliterate societies just about everybody can do just about everything, even if not equally well. Thus there is rough equality. Yet even in nonliterate societies there is always some division of labor by age and sex. In modern industrial societies, there is, in contrast to nonliterate ones (and even primarily agrarian ones), a huge number of full time-activities with a high level of specialization. It is out of the question for any one person to do everything. At first glance one might wonder why this new situation would produce inequality. Why should some occupations earn a great deal more than others? Part of the answer is that some activities are much more in demand than others. The services of a surgeon who can save your life are in greater demand than those of the man who takes the trash away from your house.

This explanation is true as far as it goes. But it is a deceptive oversimplification. There are quite a few skills that are hard to acquire, such as the writing of good sonnets, for which there is only a small demand and hence a minimal reward, at least in modern American society. To understand social demand we have to understand a society's prestige system and its ranking of different forms of human activities. We have already had occasion to notice certain broad similarities on this score. High governing officials, military officers, priests, and scientists (the latter less successfully than priests) can as a rule claim high positions of authority and prestige.

Sooner or later great wealth seems able to make its way up there too. Yet wealth as such is hardly decisive in creating the character of an elite. One need only contrast the hard-riding, hard-drinking gentlemen of eighteenth-century England with their contemporaries, the scholar officials of Imperial China, devoted to books and painting. It is fairly obvious that human societies develop collective preferences and systems of prestige that have a powerful influence on the members of that society. So far as I can see there is no useful general formula that will explain the variety of such social preferences. There are reasons for suspecting that they may reflect the outcome of earlier struggles for social recognition.

As crystallizations of past experience with a slightly contemptuous attitude toward novelty—think of the cavalry officer's attitude toward tanks—these prestige systems can be maladaptive. They can be maladaptive for other than historical reasons as well. It is impossible to account for the extremely high prestige and earnings of American stars in sports and entertainment on the basis of their contribution to social welfare or the common good, no matter how these terms are defined. A great many people want to see and hear these stars, and that is all there is to it. To sum up, social demand is important in creating and sustaining social inequality. But social demand itself changes historically and is often impossible to defend on objective grounds.

The same is obviously true of social reproduction, the last major category. Social reproduction refers to the reproduction of any given social order from one generation to the next. For the most part this reproduction takes place through the family and, especially in advanced industrial societies, also through formal and informal systems of indoctrination and education, such as peer groups, gangs, and to a lesser extent schools. The arrangements themselves vary widely from society to society and in effectiveness. Still it is probably correct to say that in the course of social reproduction there is more emphasis on indoctrination, especially indoctrination in grounds for accepting the prevailing system of inequality, than on the transmission of technical knowledge and intellectual skills. Indeed, it may not be too cynical to suggest that in modern societies a major unacknowledged purpose of formal education is to inhibit too wide a dissemination of accurate knowledge about the workings of one's own society. Partly for this reason youngsters in contemporary Western society, and perhaps elsewhere, think they are getting the "straight goods" from peer groups or selected older informants. Anything sanctioned by the older generation arouses suspicion among many adolescents. In fact, of course, indoctrination by the peer group and selected elder heroes is equally misleading, even if it seems less dull.

Inequality is widespread in the area of social reproduction. There is the authority of the father over the household and the parents over the children as well as the teacher over the students. In Europe and the United States all these forms of authority have been eroding over the past generation. There is a limit to such erosion beyond which widespread social disorder and collapse could set in. That, however, is probably less of a danger than a widespread takeover by semifascist forces of order and morality to prevent just such a collapse.

Although there are command-obedience relationships and "short" hierarchies with a few steps in the area of social reproduction, there is no single hierarchy culminating in a position near the top of the social pyramid as there often is in the case of the military, the police, and the priesthood. Only modern totalitarian dictatorships with their ministries of culture, propaganda, and education have attempted this type of top to bottom control. Even these dictatorships in practice left the family to work out the routines of daily life within a setting of a few incentives and penalties. For instance there were rewards for having children, or there were efforts to draw women into the labor force. But beyond the school curriculum there was little in the way of detailed orders from above.

At this point it is apparent that hierarchies form in connection with the working of each social function and thereby create forms of social inequality. These hierarchies arise and are sustained in two analytically distinct ways. One is by force and fraud, as in the case of a slave society that is the result of conquest. There the mechanisms of social coordination and the division of labor are forced upon the underlying slave population. The other way hierarchies can arise is a spontaneous one. In such cases individuals discover that command-obedience relationships and a division of labor are necessary to accomplish a series of socially indispensable and agreed upon tasks. In the real world, nearly all systems of social inequality have both spontaneous and compulsory features in varying amounts.

The image of social inequality presented here is not the traditional one of castes and or classes superimposed on one another in the form of a layer cake. (Since the top layer is small, the layer cake looks like a pyramid in some expositions. Or it may look like a diamond if the bottom class is also thought to be rather small.) Instead this presentation looks like a series of five ladders, corresponding to the five social functions, placed against a wall. The ladders are not equal in height. The one labeled government is generally the longest; the one labeled social reproduction the shortest. Men on the very top rungs of the governmental ladder ordinarily exercise some control or influence over affairs in all the other ladders (economic, religious, etc.). But from time to time the military and even the priesthood may become the dominant element in a society, replacing other rulers.

Each rung in each ladder represents a rank in a specific social hierarchy. In some societies it is possible for an energetic and ambitious individual to work his or, more rarely, her way to the top by changing ladders, moving from an economic ladder to a military or political one. In a rigid caste system on the other hand such a possibility does not exist, at least not in theory. Everyone is expected to stay put and occupy only the few ranks available for a particular caste.

This representation certainly acknowledges the existence of classes and castes. Individuals occupying roughly the same rank in all four social functions belong to the same social class or caste. But I hold that the separate vertical divisions reveal more about social inequality than do the concepts class and caste. The metaphor of ladders and ranks calls attention to the fact that social inequality has analytically distinguishable forms that overlap in the real life of many societies: inequalities of power, authority, wealth (including income), and prestige. It is relatively easy to convert power into authority, wealth, income, and finally prestige. It is much more difficult to convert in the reverse direction, beginning with prestige and working up to power. By itself prestige carries little weight. To last, it needs the support of some other form of inequality. With this exposition I also reject any notion that trends and social relationships in the economy always determine what happens in other parts of the social order. Often the lines of causation have run in the opposite direction. Political, military, and religious-ideological considerations have determined the contours of the economy in classical and medieval Europe and much of modern times. The same holds true for India, China, and perhaps only slightly less so for Japan. On the other hand, to my knowledge no society sufficiently "advanced" to have a written language has managed to dispense with any of these four social functions and the hierarchies necessary to make them work.

IV

Within each of the four social functions there are two analytically distinct ways by which human societies allocate individuals to unequally rewarded tasks and positions in these five hierarchies. Social scientists often refer to them as ascribed status and achieved status. From the standpoint of the individual one might call them effortless and strenuous status systems. In a system of ascribed status the individual does nothing to attain it. He or she is simply born into a high or low position. No amount of effort can raise the individual to a higher position, though disapproved behavior can lead to the loss of high status. A hereditary nobility is a familiar example from the top of the social scale. Another from the bottom is the lower caste (or outcaste) Hindu, where the work of the males brings them in contact with garbage, human excrement, corpses and dead animals. Nothing the individual can do will enable a person to rise out of this caste. In theory a caste system contains only ascribed or effortless status. In practice, however, even caste societies display some touches of upward and downward mobility or achieved status.

Achieved status one could call the strenuous status because the individual ordinarily must make strenuous efforts to attain higher status as well as to avoid falling into a lower position. In the case of achieved status, the society through its appointed "gate-keeping" officials confers high position on the basis of socially valued and publicly demonstrated capacities. Often these highly valued capacities may lack any close connection with the duties required of a person of high standing.

The mandarinate in the Chinese Empire is one of the best known examples. Chinese scholar-officials were recruited on the basis of knowledge of the Chinese classics, as demonstrated in examinations. These classics contain a great deal of moral preaching supported by historical anecdote. The main thing the officials learned from their preparation was how to produce acceptable rhetoric, no easy task given the behavior of many an emperor. Others learned how to play power politics, and a few managed to perceive fairly accurately the economic and political problems facing China.

Still, the reason for the tremendous effort put into acquiring literary culture was to get a good job. In theory any male could apply. On the other hand the long years of study meant that only those with property to support them stood any chance of success. Rich people with no children or a clutch of academic dullards sometimes adopted a bright boy hoping that he could bring fame and fortune to the family or at least keep it going as a credit to the ancestors. Thus the mandarinate was in theory a set of purely achieved statuses, while in practice there was a substantial ascribed or hereditary component.

All forms of achieved status, I suspect, have a large ascribed component. It is difficult to think of any society where the experiences of living in the lower classes are actually helpful to achieving membership in the upper ranks of one of the four functional hierarchies. To be sure many a political leader finds it helpful to have the common touch, an intuitive understanding of how ordinary people think and feel, based on some direct experience. Such different examples as Julius Caesar, Louis XIV, Lenin, and Mao come to mind in this connection. But the common touch is only a touch of lower-class culture in which other elements of a socially formed personality predominate overwhelmingly. As the talented move up the social pyramid, they usually shed the traces of lower-class origins and are liable to be embarrassed by any that stubbornly cling to them.

Though Imperial China constitutes a decisive exception, we generally think of the effortless and ascribed inequalities as flourishing mainly in stable agrarian societies and achieved status as being mainly a product of the ferment that accompanies industrialization and modernization. The contrast makes reasonably good sense, although the top military and political positions in classical Athens and in Rome seem on the basis of limited evidence, to have gone to men of talent, luck, and background in proportions not very different from those prevailing in twentieth-century Europe. At least in the short run political disorder may do more to loosen up a rigid class system than economic growth.

On the other hand the introduction of substantial amounts of money into an agrarian society always corrodes the traditional social hierarchy. Enough money in the hands of a parvenu will sooner or later buy the offices and honors traditionally reserved for members of the dominant class on the basis of their traditional virtues, such as a somewhat antiquated military skill requiring much bravery, control of "orthodox" religious and cultural symbols, and finally just plain snobbery based on inherited status. When it becomes possible to purchase the status because aristocrats and aristocratic governments generally run short of cash with the onset of modernization, snobbery becomes futile. As the barriers to the ascent of the rich parvenu begin to come down, premodern elites are likely to dig in their heels. The cultural expression of this move takes the form of an emphasis on old-fashioned virtues: loyalty to superiors, bravery, hard work for the peasants. These virtues appear within the framework of an organic society, that is one without class struggle, and where every person knows his place in a set of organically related social activities. This romantic conservatism contrasts the alleged organic unity of the premodern society with the supposed destruction of traditional family and community life in the cities, a destruction supposedly due to the ruthless pursuit of money. There is just enough truth in this romantic ideology, and quite enough need for the comfort of its message, to keep the doctrine very much alive, now and for the foreseeable future.

There are considerable variations in the intensity and forms of the conflicts arising out of the introduction of trade and monetary relationships into a static agrarian economy. Here it is impossible to do more than hint at the differences. The United States found itself in a civil war with its agrarian slaveholder elite, even though this elite was thoroughly capitalist (and certainly not feudal). England may have had the easiest time of all, possibly because the landed classes had engaged in commercial undertakings for a long time. By the eighteenth century, anyone who had money and wit would find an easy acceptance in the ruling elite. China, by way of contrast, has had an unusually painful time. When around the turn of the century it began to be possible to buy a degree and thereby short circuit the onerous trial by examination, the whole edifice of Confucian morality, indeed the whole moral justification of the existing order showed itself to have crumbled away. Men and women lost their social attachments and found themselves adrift on a dark sea of stormy despair with a few flashes of light from utopian hopes that in time produced their own disappointments.

This emotional turmoil should not blind us to the fact that modern industrial societies stress the importance of skills in allocating jobs and social positions to a degree unheard of in pre-industrial societies. The rise of the professions is strictly a feature of modern societies. The emphasis on technical competence as the basis for getting and holding a job is not limited to the professions. Airplane pilots have to demonstrate this competence. So do electronics technicians, as well as others in less demanding occupations. To an outsider who observes the incompetent and reckless behavior of, say, drivers of huge trailer trucks, or who follows the details of reports on airplane and spacecraft accidents, the level of competence often seems abysmally low. Nevertheless an applicant has to demonstrate *some* skill. He or she does not get the job merely on the basis of social background.

A more important observation is that those who merely pass tests seldom if ever find their way to the top of the heap. If they do get to the top, their technical training, even in the case of lawyers, plays only a minor role. Administrative skills, the ability to persuade, cajole, impress, and threaten people in such a way that tasks get done in a coordinated fashion, are the qualities necessary to get to the top. Furthermore a visible political leader must know how to play on popular emotions. In that sense we are still ruled by amateurs who call on professionals with special skills when they think the skills might help, often to buttress a position or policy that is the outcome of political infighting and synthetically manufactured public outrage.

The introduction of tests for competence arouses the opposition of upper-class groups accustomed to having access to these posts as a privilege of their class. The history of appointments to bureaucratic office in the government and of military officers in England, France, and Germany during the eighteenth century and well into the nineteenth century displays the struggle against "merit" quite clearly. Once the standards have been adopted complaints begin that they are too high, biased toward certain groups in the society and against others, or unfair in other ways. The insiders in other words try to set up a monopoly while the outsiders try to force the gate. Many of the outsiders come from the lower strata. In modern societies it seems almost impossible to establish a system of social inequality that can command really widespread assent. Yet inequality is probably more "socially necessary" than ever before.

In modern capitalist societies specific public demonstrations of competence for specific jobs and occupations play an important though still secondary role. Prestige and high status are indeed matters of achievement, often by strenuous effort, in these societies. But the achievement is not tied to a specific occupation. The visible sign is merit as demonstrated in the market place, or the acquisition of wealth by more or less legal methods. Though the acquisition of wealth leads to comfort, luxury, and a substantial amount of social approbation, in the course of the twentieth century it has seemed less and less satisfactory as the primary goal of human existence. An extreme form of this rejection appeared in the 1960s and 1970s as Western societies witnessed a widespread adolescent revolt against not only meritocratic requirements but the general standards and taste of upper-middle-class culture. As part of their revolt they adopted what they believed to be the dress, manners, and ideas of the oppressed including a big dose of ethnocentrism and cultural provincialism. It is unlikely that this adolescent upheaval would have taken place on so wide a scale without the stimulus of American military intervention in Vietnam, which outraged more and more adults, inclining them toward tolerance of rebellious adolescents. Whether this discontent with, and even hostility towards, both capitalism and liberalism, a hostility that has both idealistic and quite selfish sources, will some day seriously undermine the motivation and commitments that keep capitalist societies going remains to be seen. In any case, it is by now reasonably clear that capitalist societies are not as badly off as socialist ones on the score of their moral authority and legitimacy.

V

Now we may turn from variations in the way human societies allocate individuals to specific slots in a set of more or less unequally ordered activities, to variations in the authority, prestige, and perquisites that these four social functions have been able to command in different historical epochs. For the purpose at hand it will be sufficient to draw attention to some changes in the control of violence and of the unknown.

To begin with a familiar but instructive case, prior to about 1940 the military played at best a tertiary role in American society. Their rise to prominence as perhaps the dominant partner in the military-industrial complex was due to the Second World War. To explain this change in the character of American society it is necessary to look outside the boundaries of the United States itself. Similar changes have occurred in many instances and are by no means limited to modern times. Athens emerged into recorded history as a nation of peasant warriors. The Persian Wars turned it into a naval empire with strong trading and colonial interests.

It is worthwhile emphasizing that transformations in the human institutions that organize, control, and use violence are by no means wholly predetermined by economic factors. Instead military and police organizations often determine what happens in the economy. To paraphrase Marx, we can say that the social relations of death are frequently more important than the social relations of production.

Turning now to changes in the control of moral symbolism, and fears of the unknown, we see in European society from the Middle Ages onward an equally profound but rather more gradual set of changes. In the Middle Ages this control was a near monopoly of the Catholic Church. Amid the multiple terrors and teeming uncertainties of life on earth the Catholic Church offered the comfort and consolation of salvation after death. Hence the faithful should not be overly concerned with present suffering. Guilt the Church assuaged with what became a highly bureaucratized system of organized forgiveness. It resembled the automat-cafeteria of depression times. One put coins in the slot and out came the "dessert" in the form of authorized forgiveness and penance.

Nowadays this function of managing the unknown and the unpredictable (as well as taking care of guilt) has split into numerous subdivisions. There are the natural scientists. Then there are the educators. In addition there are numerous varieties of moral exhorters and advisers, who share television, radio, and the newspaper with entertainers, from whom they are not always easy to distinguish. Cultural and ethical standards have become fragmented to the point where there are almost as many varieties of morality as breakfast foods in a supermarket. If there is any visible principle of change in this area, it would seem to be Herbert Spencer's theory of evolutionary change from homogeneity to heterogeneity.

Now we may ask whether there is any general principle that could help us to understand changes in the power, authority, and prestige of different social functions and the social groups that perform them. Marxism provided an answer that seems to me helpful but insufficient. I suggest that changes in the social usefulness of such functions, changes that come about from both domestic and foreign causes or a combination of the two, can go a long way toward accounting for such shifts in the structure of inequality. However, it is no simple matter to sort out the empirical evidence in specific cases. Furthermore there are built-in traps in the evidence that may easily mislead the unwary. For instance the term "useful" can conceal as much as it reveals. We have to ask "useful to whom" and whether there are harmful consequences for others.

To elaborate a bit, in "civilized" societies there is generally a contest, usually but not always peaceful, for esteem and a share in material goods. The contest, as I perceive it, includes the class struggle where one exists, but is much broader. It is simultaneously a contest among social functions as well as ranks within each function. The higher strata are generally more active in this contest than the lower ones, though they too enter the fray from time to time thereby making the contest more intense. Meanwhile threats come and go from other societies and often alter greatly the calculations and strategies of those engaged in the domestic struggles: All this tugging and hauling, which at times degenerates into violently destructive conflict, is as old as civilized life. For roughly the last five centuries it has been going on in a context of economic and moral change where familiar social landmarks disappear and old rules of conduct cease to make sense. The rate and depth of change have both greatly increased

in modern times. Yet one can see intermittent signs of change and diso-
rientation in human societies just about as far back as the records go.
Thus human societies are constantly changing in response to internal
pressures and external threats. In any given society the organization of
inequality undergoes important changes in adapting to the threats just
mentioned and simultaneously creating new ones. The organization of
inequality constitutes the sum of all social adaptations up to a given point
in time. It sets the limit within which most members of society live. Still
if a large enough body of people, and a strategically placed one, come to
the conclusion that, for example, a certain military ethic and style are no
longer useful, then it will suffer. The same is true of a religious or
economic ethic. Since none of these are watertight intellectual or social
compartments, changes in one will have consequences for the others. Ex-
aggerating slightly we can say that with the passage of time the normal
assumption of utility dissolves into a judgment of futility. A specific form
of inequality becomes historically obsolete.

A judgment of futility seldom goes quite as far as the term suggests, at
least not in its socially accepted and politically significant form. A judgment of futility may or may not be the beginning of—or any part of—a
wholesale transformation of the prevailing system of social inequality and
the set of values that sustains it. What actually happens depends on the
social and cultural context that requires concrete analysis in each case. The
British cavalry officer of the eighteenth and nineteenth centuries, the Japanese samurai and the Prussian Junkers of the same period show different
assessments of survival value in a presumably obsolete social formation.
Likewise kings lasted beyond the First World War despite the regicides
of the seventeenth and eighteenth centuries.

The main difficulty and the most serious source of error in analyzing
any concrete case of social obsolescence derives from a circularity built
into the evidence. Those with high status in any society do their best to
see to it that the qualities they possess are the ones upon which their
society will place a high value. Thus one cannot say that such and such a
group enjoys high status because it performs a function highly valued in
this society. A statement like this is no more than a deceptive tautology,
a way of succumbing to the mystique of a particular elite. It is necessary
to demonstrate by independent means that this ostensibly highly valued
social task really is of great importance, that there would be serious loss
and suffering if it were discontinued or its performance reduced. Such
evidence is hard to obtain but not impossible.

VI

The issues of exploitation and oppression have already appeared in the foregoing discussion of the main social causes of inequality. The concluding portion of this essay will analyze the extent to which exploitation and oppression may or may not be unavoidable features of any system of inequality. For that purpose I will first sketch out what I trust is not a totally unrealistic model of an inegalitarian society with little or no exploitation. Then we may see how and why such a society could generate strong exploitative and oppressive traits. In the light of this somewhat cheerless conclusion we will then change tacks to approach the problems with different questions. We shall ask what obstacles exist to the establishment of an egalitarian society, posing the issue mainly in terms of modern society.

To sketch a model of an inegalitarian society without exploitation or oppression it is only necessary to stress practices and tendencies that have existed at one time or another in quite a number of societies. There is no need to create another imaginary utopia. Instead we are looking for the conditions that promote the acceptance of more or less rational authority by subordinate elements in the population.

Ordinarily the subordinate strata have quite specific expectations about what their rulers should do for them. They expect from their rulers protection against foreign attack. Likewise they expect protection against domestic predators in the form of thieves and bandits. Where the central authority is remote and ineffective, the people will try to protect themselves. If the local representatives of power are themselves greedy and exploitative and the bandits choose local elites as their favorite targets, large sections of the population may side with the bandits. By that point, however, the established powers are in serious trouble.

Maintaining domestic peace and order includes the settling of disputes according to a generally acceptable code of justice. What makes a code acceptable is the prospect that the little man can get his due if he is in the right legally and morally. In practice that situation appears to be rare. Many older legal codes do not recognize it even in theory. Instead the severity of punishment depends on the social status of the victim. Yet the hope that disputes may be worked out according to a code has been important in the past. In the twentieth century it seems more powerful and widespread.

A satisfactorily working economy is another precondition for the popular acceptance of authority. A satisfactory economy exists where most people can obtain enough material goods to sustain their accustomed social roles. An unsatisfactory economy deprives people of their accustomed status. The belief that the ruler or rulers are responsible for the economic security of the population is strong even in preindustrial societies. In contemporary industrial societies it is even stronger. As in China under "good" emperors, the ruler may be expected to help people who suffer from natural disasters, especially crop failures due to flood or drought. Serious and widespread economic failure undermines the ruler's legitimacy. This is the case in the United States as well as in China.

Thus the relation between rulers and rules, dominant and subordinate strata takes the form of an implicit or sometimes explicit social contract. If rulers provide protection, justice, and a satisfactory economy, they fulfill their part of the contract. The subordinate population will then carry out their part by yielding a substantial economic surplus to the dominant elements in the social order and remaining peaceable. If that were all, we could say that in such situations there was little or no exploitation. But it is far from the whole story.

Authority displays a built in tendency toward abuse and selfish aggrandizement even where it is for the most part rational. By that, I mean where it serves generally accepted nonpredatory social purposes. It is rather obvious that authority is widely and even enthusiastically accepted when its purposes are predatory against other societies *and* successful. Self-aggrandizement takes the cancer-like growth of governmental and private institutions well beyond any imaginable social necessity for them. Internal security organs in socialist states are the most familiar example. Some form of internal police is necessary in any modern society. It only takes one bad criminal to make a police system necessary. But once established any form of bureaucracy tries to grow. One reason for growth is the extreme difficulty in deciding in any specific case what is superfluous and what is not, even if the distinction obviously exists. There is a limit to the amount of resources a society can afford to give to, say, a department of agriculture. Members of an organization will push for an institution's growth because at least a few believe in its mission, while others want more and better jobs. The tendency toward self-propelled growth increases inequality. On occasion it may also produce oppression. Abuse takes the form of using authority or power for personal gain at the expense of members of the public. Using official position to demand goods, services, sexual favors and the like, which are not part of the legal and customary demands of the office, constitute widespread examples. Many a modern city, where one has to get official permission to do just about anything from disposing of trash to holding a parade, offers splendid opportunities for petty gouging with fees for licenses and permissions.

Such situations have often grown up in pre-industrial societies, though it is not confined to them. The usual justification for such petty gouging is that the government is too poor to pay many minor officials who must therefore supplement their earnings by shady methods. This justification is based on dubious assumptions. One is that minor officials will become honest if they are paid more. The experience of the decline of administrative corruption in England during the nineteenth century suggests, on the other hand, that new methods of recruitment and the concomitant growth of new ethical standards are equally necessary. The justification also assumes that a pre-industrial government's resources for paying officials and the officials' conceptions of a satisfactory income are both fixed quantities. That is true at any given moment in time. Over a longer period, say a generation or more, both quantities can change a great deal. Relatively honest government, though rare, is possible. Again as English experience shows it can emerge out of a history of corrupt abuse. To bring it about apparently requires a cultural and social mutation similar to the triumph of Victorian moral standards over those of the eighteenth century. This triumph was a reworking of old ideas, mainly Christian ones, in the new social and economic context of advancing industrialism. The situation demanded calculation, foresight, hard work, and control of impulses and instincts, and yet permitted touches of tender conscience. In such situations, admonition and exhortation, especially by foreigners, produce by themselves negligible results.

There are at least two more innate sources of inequality and, on occasion, oppression that are liable to afflict regimes with egalitarian commitments. Both concern relationships between dominant and subordinate groups. Both appear to be necessary for the successful exercise of power and authority. One is the role of fear, including fear in even a most benign regime. The other is the fragmentation of the underlying population in relation to the holders of power and authority.

Without any fear behind it, authority ceases to be effective. If authority can be challenged at will, even in apparently harmless ways such as graffiti, without some kind of retribution, sooner or later it will cease to be taken seriously and therefore disappear.

As a matter of historical fact there has nearly always been some element of force and fraud in the way ruling groups obtain and maintain power. This situation has usually been enough to elicit easily the minimum dose of fear necessary to hold the regime together, and often a great deal more than the minimum dose. If however a government is obeyed mainly due to fear, then that government and its remaining supporters are in serious trouble. Some element of fear well short of this extreme or terminal situation apparently characterizes every political system.

There is another aspect of fear that requires mention. Any "normally" strong government can always mobilize overwhelming force in short order against any challenge to its authority. Indeed the ability to crush such a challenge amounts to a definition of a strong government. A regime that cannot mobilize enough resources to put down a challenge, and strike fear into the hearts of those sympathetic to the challenge, is automatically dismissed as weak and ineffectual. Even a regime based almost entirely on accepted rational grounds for its authority—something hard to find except perhaps in some sheltered political backwater—has to be willing and able to use force and instill fear because in a good-sized society there is always the possibility that a tiny but audacious minority will challenge the moral authority of the state. The challenge need not be political. It may be no more than a criminal gang. Such challenges are always tiny at the start. Yet under the right circumstances they can attract more and more adherents. Both pre-industrial and modern states have tolerated disorder and the flouting of established authority on a wide scale. Still there is a limit to what a state can tolerate and remain a state. Indeed if the challengers can meet and *create* needs relevant to the historical epoch, they can replace existing rulers—with the help of their own varieties of fraud and violence.

The second precondition that encourages oppression concerns the social structure of the lower strata. The disunity of subordinate strata relative to the dominant strata helps to sustain "legitimate" political systems, and even more, those with marked oppressive and exploitative features. As Gaetano Mosca pointed out long ago, a dominant minority enjoys great advantages simply because it is a minority. For that reason it can organize and act much more easily. The mass of the population contains so many diverse interest groups that action becomes extremely difficult.

It is worth noticing on the other hand that ethnic and religious minorities also organize more easily than the general population because they too are minorities that can coalesce around certain symbols. As long as they are in opposition, these minorities are rather successful in using their collective symbols to overcome cleavages within the minority derived from class and occupational differences. By the last decade of the twentieth century minorities in many parts of the world were channeling their grievances into nationalist demands. Nationalism provides for these peoples an explanation and remedy for their misfortunes with a far greater popular appeal than Marxism ever had. If they succeed there may be worse cruelty than before.

The subordinate population in modern industrial societies is rather more differentiated than was the case with the preindustrial monarchies that flourished in Europe and Asia during the seventeenth century and well into the eighteenth. There the subordinate population was made up mainly of peasants and artisans. To be sure there were important subdivisions in each. With the advent of industry the number of new occupations greatly increased while many old ones changed rather than disappeared. We now have big commercial farmers, new forms of artisans (such as plumbers, electricians, mechanics, and miscellaneous repair services), sales clerks, office workers, factory workers, and so forth, each with a distinct set of insecurities and demands on the social order. It is tempting to assert that we live in a mass society without real masses (or at least homogeneous masses) just as we live in a service economy without adequate services.

As modern society becomes more complex, the vulnerability of society as a whole to the failure of any one of its working parts becomes ever greater. The consequence is that the workforce in any key sector, if it is able to act collectively, can hold the rest of society up for ransom by refusing to work. So far such attempts on the scale of a whole industry have been rare. Since World War II we have had a rail strike in England that helped produce the victory of Margaret Thatcher. The success of French students in almost paralyzing de Gaulle's regime was a similar situation, though one that also reveals the vulnerability of modern governments to political disorder. In these instances the groups that tried to hold up the society in order to force through their demands used at least some of the rhetoric of class struggle. The leaders claimed that their demands were the just demands of the unfortunate and oppressed and that they were acting not only on behalf of their own followers but on behalf of the unfortunate and oppressed generally.

How seriously should one take such claims? The outcome of a class struggle is, in theory at least, supposed to be a gain for most people. It would be hard to maintain that such was the situation or intention here. Rather it looks like a war of all against all in which one contestant can use a strategic advantage to levy tribute on all the others. In the short run it is a zero-sum contest insofar as what the winner gains everyone else loses. Furthermore I would suggest that this has become the main pattern of conflict in present-day societies, capitalist or communist. Every contestant wants more jobs, higher pay, and less hard work.

If this impression is correct, it means that oppression and exploitation have become much more democratic than was the case in pre-industrial societies. It is no longer just the dominant class that can exploit and oppress. All sorts of people can find ways to do it now, though of course not everybody. In both capitalist and the remaining socialist societies the rhetoric of class struggle serves to justify group struggles for quite selfish ends.

Summing up the observation on the lower strata we find three factors that promote various forms of exploitation and oppression even where such tendencies are minimal to begin with. They are fear of the rulers, the rulers' ability to mount overwhelming force at any single point, and finally the fragmentation of the lower strata, a situation especially noticeable in contemporary industrial societies. The systems of authority, or of social coordination from above are an even more important source of inequality and, potentially, of oppression. Even the most rational forms of authority are subject to corruption, abuse, and unjustifiable expansion of facilities and perquisites.

In closing we may ask what obstacles the members of a civilized society would have to overcome in order to establish an egalitarian social order and the problems an egalitarian order would have to solve to maintain itself. Two comments must be made to clear the ground.

It is possible to accept as a fact a very unequal distribution of talents and capacities among human beings without accepting this form of inequality as more than a minor cause of social inequality. The inequalities manifest in social institutions and perpetuated through them have pri-. marily social and historical causes rather than biological ones. If, on the other hand, it should be possible to set up an egalitarian society that was at the same time quite fair in allocating individuals to different tasks, considerable inequality would presumably appear within a generation or so.

My second comment is on the Christian left's attempt to accept a considerable degree of inequality in modern industrial societies while drawing the sting of this inequality with a generous application of Christian balm. According to this judgment, well expressed in R. H. Tawney's *Equality*, the ways in which human beings are alike are more important than the ways in which they become unequal. We share many of the same feelings and something like a common propensity to misfortune and a common capacity for joy.

This element of shared humanity provides the basis for arguments on behalf of at least minimal civility and decency (i.e., avoiding cruelty) in the treatment of any human being. Yet, it is only too painfully obvious that in practice this minimal civility and decency is the exception rather than the rule. By itself the belief in a common humanity has little effect. To be effective it requires the help of other beliefs and social arrangements.

Thus neither the biological argument against the possibility of equality nor the ethical one favoring this possibility carry much conviction. Apparently one has to start from scratch.

To establish and sustain an egalitarian society it would be necessary to do three things. First, one would have to overcome or at least neutralize the historical results of force and fraud in creating special privileges for the dominant elements of the society. In a good many cases the mere prospect of such a purge would be enough to set off a civil war. The second task would be to find methods of social coordination that did not depend on authority or relationships of command and obedience. As discussed earlier, the market does provide through the price system a series of decentralized incentives and negative sanctions that together create a fair facsimile of voluntary acts resulting in social cooperation without any central authority. However the market has never been able to generate, and probably never could generate, all the goods and services in modern societies. Its role is minimal, for instance, in the provision of such different services as the military and education. Clearly there is a range of activities in which price alone is insufficient to elicit the desired form of behavior.

Furthermore, even within the range of activities coordinated by the market authority and its resulting inequalities, authority often plays a decisive role. Management has to obtain capital, turn it into machinery, and then direct, cajole, or order specifiable types of workers to serve the machinery with raw materials in such a way as to turn out serviceable goods. Where the cues of price variation, including the price of labor, are weak or meaningless, as has been the case in socialist societies, the resort to bureaucratic compulsion has been unavoidable. Appeals to an alleged socialist conscience have been ineffective in comparison with fear and material self-interest.

The third obstacle to an egalitarian society derives from the division of labor. An elaborate division of labor into numerous types and grades of skill, ranging from eye surgeons to trash collectors, is an inherent characteristic of modern industrial societies. The serious egalitarian would have to find a way to recruit, train, allocate, and motivate each of these different kinds of labor without resorting to differences in pay, or at most using very small differences. To state the problem is enough to show that it is just about insoluble short of a near total destruction of modern society. Even if, as pointed out earlier, the capitalist division of labor and corresponding system of rewards display many irrationalities, an egalitarian one is hardly the remedy, and looks like an impossibility if taken at all seriously.

Quite apart from any historical legacy of force and fraud in the establishment of social inequalities, modern societies generate and reproduce inequalities out of the need for authority and social coordination and as a consequence of the division of labor. For these reasons alone social inequalities will almost certainly be with us for the foreseeable future.

* * * * *

This prediction does not carry any implication that one should passively accept the world as it is and is likely to be. The assertion that inequality is a permanent feature of complex human societies is not meant to justify any existing form of inequality.

How then can one distinguish between justifiable and unjustifiable forms of inequality? The question is not an easy one. Religious and political doctrines have justified just about every conceivable form of inequality as part of some natural or divine order. There is not much help to be found grubbing around in those archives. We would do better, I believe, to toss this intellectual freight overboard since the ship is already leaking at the seams, and try for a simple commonsense solution.

The test for any given form of inequality is not whether it fits some higher "cosmic" scheme of the universe and the nature of human affairs or human society therein. Instead the question to ask is whether this inequality is required in order to elicit concretely specifiable and socially necessary goods and services. For instance, is a salary of $200,000 a year required to have the services of a cardiac surgeon? And how valuable are these services to the society at large when set against the known needs of the society? Such questions, it must be emphasized, cannot have completely objective and determinate answers, partly because they require comparing an unknown future situation with currently existing realities. The results of such a test would still leave plenty of room for disputes over the distribution of resources. Nevertheless one can trace out the causes and consequences of an existing form of inequality with enough accuracy to make worthwhile judgments about the wisdom of leaving the situation as it stands or attempting some changes. Granting the element of indeterminacy in such discussions, I still cannot discern any reason for letting the status quo have the benefit of all doubts.

Rational Discussion: Comparative Historical Notes on Its Origins, Enemies, and Prospects

I

By rational discussion I mean a discussion, debate, or peaceable argument among two or more individuals facing an important and difficult issue. They try to persuade one another primarily by means of logic and evidence. Though the issue may be an emotional one—a matter to be discussed more fully in a moment—in a discussion that deserves to be called rational, the participants keep emotional and personal appeals to a minimum. They refrain from personal abuse. The assumption is that those with different opinions deserve respect and serious intellectual consideration. Lurking in the background here is a rough notion of human equality, or perhaps more accurately the social equality of all people capable of rational thought and behavior. Those deemed incapable are excluded.

This conception of rational discussion is an ideal type in Max Weber's terminology, an abstraction formed in the hope of clarifying a messy and impure reality. It is also an idealization—some might say a romantic idealization—of certain ways of coping with disagreement that probably have never existed in quite so edifying a form. Nor is there much reason to expect purely dispassionate and rational discussion to be a common feature of human history. Political change hardly ever takes place without arousing intense passions. Nevertheless victory does not necessarily go to those with the most indignation or moral outrage. Without a cool and detached assessment of the existing situation, the opportunities it presents as well as those it closes off, no political movement can be victorious. It cannot even survive for long. Here is where rational discussion comes in. When rational discussion works, it brings all the feasible choices to the surface so that the participants in the discussion can choose among them.

If rational analysis and rational discussion remain indispensable even in a highly charged political situation, they probably work better in less highly charged contexts. These include discussions about the application of well-known scientific principles in the natural or "hard" sciences. If the application of the natural sciences is relatively uncontroversial, the foundations and basic concepts are still matters of sharp dispute. The notion that history and the social sciences are controversial while mathematics and the hard sciences are free from debate and quarrels is a pure myth. The foundations of mathematics have been a matter of sharp and at times acrid dispute since the latter part of the seventeenth century.[1] In the case of physics it seems to this outsider that the foundations are just as wobbly, but the discussions are much better tempered.

Often, academic discussions are acrimonious and boring in a way that leads to a consensus of exhaustion rather than real agreement. Yet decisions have to be made and judgments passed. For that reason, at least in economically advanced countries, one rarely hears the proposal that attempts at rational discussion be abandoned. Judgment by *diktat* in the name of a dubious doctrine or ephemeral popular mood is the only alternative to attempts at rational discussion. Right now hardly anyone wants that.

II

While the ideal may never have been realized, there have been approaches to it, as well as outright and vehement rejections. These very different postures toward the theory and practice of rational discussion have had great and grave consequences for human happiness and human misery.

Some of the early sprouts of what much later became the working institutions of rational discussion appear in ancient Athens. Pericles' Funeral Oration celebrates Athenian freedom of thought, taste, and speech as well as the city's military power. On the other hand Pericles saw to it that the issue of his strategy in the war against Sparta did not come before

---

[1]On mathematics see Morris Kline, *Mathematics: The Loss of Certainty* (New York, 1980); on physics there is enlightening first-hand information in Albert Einstein and Max Born, *Briefwechsel 1916–1955* (Munich, 1969).

the assembly. Evidently as Pericles saw the situation, the Athenian assembly was no place to expect a sensible discussion of his essentially defensive policy. That policy was hard on the peasants because it led to annual Spartan invasions and the destruction of crops. Perhaps wisely Pericles preferred to impose silence instead of allowing public discussion of a very touchy issue. To judge from later debates in the assembly it seems unlikely that a public debate on the policy of Pericles could have been rational.

Nor is it easy to guess what Pericles himself might have meant by rational discussion. In his day as well as afterward the notions of rational discussion and rational policy were latent rather than explicit and lacked any clear referent. Especially after the death of Pericles the situation was one in which every political leader could claim that his policy was the rational one because it would bring glory and other advantages to the city. In Thucydides' thinking, on the other hand, one can see a clear distinction emerging. The distinction is between demagogic political appeals and nondemagogic ones. Demagogic appeals were those that sought popular support with minimal attention to their risks and probable costs. Almost certainly, a good many Athenian citizens besides Thucydides were aware of demagogy and were uneasy about its consequences. Indeed it is hardly an exaggeration to assert that Plato and Aristotle in their different ways were trying to find out how to establish a *polis* without demagogy— and one in which their version of rational discussion could flourish.

In the next century Demosthenes was the leading political figure. Unlike Pericles, who died long before the Spartan victory, Demosthenes had the misfortune to live long enough to witness the disastrous failure of his efforts to rouse the Athenians against the dangers of Macedon. In Demosthenes' speeches there is considerable reliance on facts and logic. There was at least the hope—not just a pretense—that the facts and logic of the situation as he presented them would be compelling and rouse the Athenians to action before it was too late.

But Demosthenes' conclusions came prior to his logic. Anyone who did not share his political conclusions was, for Demosthenes, not worth talking to, or worse, probably a traitor who had sold his tongue for Macedonian bribes. It is of course impossible to argue with anyone who sees a conspiracy behind every disagreement. At that time, just before the final end of Athenian independence, the political situation as a whole was highly unfavorable to the development of a system of rational discourse. With the presuppositions that Demosthenes expressed about his opponents, presuppositions and accusations that may have been quite true, rational discourse was simply out of the question. The situation was too tense, the alternatives too stark.

Whether Athenian legal practice, so far as we can know it from surviving records, came closer to rational discussion is really a question for specialists. Since it is well known that public speakers could get training in how to make any argument look plausible — an idea that runs exactly counter to modern concepts of rational discussion, where one strips away all forms of self-deception for the sake of truth, honesty, and a valid conclusion — it seems somewhat unlikely that the legal contribution could have been very great. Nevertheless the Athenians did develop — if they did not create — an adversary system of legal practice. A peaceful and socially controlled adversary relationship is a significant component in the development of rational discussion. Plato made this relationship central to his dialogues. Even the theater may have helped ordinary citizens understand the notion of getting to the heart of a matter by listening to the viewpoints of opposing sides. Under the fateful name of dialectic this mode of thinking was to enjoy a long career in philosophy.

The theory and practice of discussion as a way of problem solving and avoiding or resolving conflicts took still other forms among these inventive and loquacious people. Somewhere Max Weber pointed out that the Greeks wanted to find a form of argument that could really put the bite on an opponent and compel assent. Logic and mathematics, first rationalized and systematized by the Greeks, do exactly that. With the acceptance of simple "undeniable" (we know better now) premises one could lead an intellectual opponent to inescapable conclusions. To the modern romantic this mathematical and logical thinking sounds horribly authoritarian. In classical Greece that was not true. Mathematics and logic provided tools that for the first time made it possible to compel assent from anybody: emperor, king, priest or general. High social status had nothing to do with truth or argument. Thus the mathematical-rational point of view and democracy were bound together and mutually supportive.

Still, there was something missing in all these moves toward rational discussion. It was the absence of any control over partisanship in the interest of truth. This gap was apparent in the workings of the legal system. The jurors of Athens, composed of citizens who could afford the time and who welcomed the small fee for jury duty, were notorious for seeking their own entertainment rather than rendering justice.

Looking back over the Athenian record in solving human problems by rational discussion, we can see that the most important aspect of this record was the fact that it was a distinct historical novelty. In the course of bloody internal conflicts the Athenians managed to create the world's first democracy in a civilized state. If they were going to have a democracy at all, the citizens would have to learn to try persuasion and to give up force, at least in politics among equals. Unlike the military theocracies that preceded her, there was in Athens no supreme authority with an army, a bureaucracy, or a priesthood to make decisions and issue orders for the people to execute. Athenians would have to decide on the orders for themselves. Some of the persuasion would have to be rational and a great deal more would have to seem rational. In comparison with its historical predecessors Athenian efforts look like both a qualitative leap forward *and* a return to the ways of debate in the tribal councils of some nonliterate and simpler societies.

Imperial China had some of the cultural prerequisites for rational discussion, though the distribution of power and authority in China was almost the opposite of that in the democratic phase of ancient Athens. In political and religious issues, literate Chinese followed for the most part the maxim *jamais trop de zèle* before Talleyrand tried to make this a diplomatic principle. To be sure there were occasional attacks on the Buddhists, and especially their monasteries, when these began to look like a state within a state. But there was little theological fervor behind these attacks. China lacked enthusiasm in the older religious sense of the word. Confucianism eschewed the supernatural and was not really a religion despite its support of ancestor worship. It was mainly a system of etiquette. Its main competitor, Taoism, had a strong streak of anti-political quietism. Chinese culture, though capable of xenophobia like practically all human cultures, was not one to generate heresy hunting. In that sense it favored rational discussion.

The Confucian tradition also carried, especially in the works of Mencius, the general notion of an obligation to criticize and correct unjust authority or manifestly destructive policies pursued by such an authority. This concept of the right and obligation to criticize is of course fundamental to rational discussion, even if by itself insufficient to ensure it. It is insufficient because it says nothing about the tone and etiquette of discussion. As we have seen, however, that Confucian ideal of a gentleman strongly opposed any form of vehement partisanship. On that score Chinese culture appears more favorable to rational discussion than Athenian.

Unlike the culture of public oratory in democratic Athens authoritarian China operated through a memorandum culture. Offhand one might think that this situation would have encouraged the development of rational debate in China because a memorandum culture provides hardly any opportunities for demagogues. Yet a memorandum culture limits the opportunities for dialogue. The only person who may be persuaded by a memorandum is the person designated to read it. Here was the main obstacle. The only worthwhile recipient for an official document in China was the emperor himself or, second best, an official (sometimes a eunuch) whom the emperor trusted and believed.

At this point the imperial system failed badly. Critical reporting and advice were fairly effective under good emperors, that is when they were hardly necessary. Under bad emperors, interested in their own expensive pleasures rather than the welfare of the people, critical reporting and advice were worse than useless. The emperor disregarded the advice and punished its authors for seditious disrespect. Outside the mandarinate there were no effective interest groups that could push an emperor in the direction of behaving himself or adopting good policies against his inclinations. In turn the mandarinate itself was fragmented into factions and ultimately impotent. To put the point more broadly, the authoritarian structure of the Chinese empire greatly inhibited any exchange of differing opinions, whether or not the discussion was based on logic and evidence.

III

With our soundings into two very different cultures, ancient Athens and imperial China, let us see if they might reveal or suggest social situations favorable and unfavorable to the habit of rational discussion that could apply to other times and places.

To perceive the magnitude of the Athenian achievement, one has to see it against the background of the great theocratic monarchies of the Near East that preceded it. Athenian society was very different indeed. Just how and why the differences arose is hard to determine because there is little evidence. Some historians have thrown up their hands in wonder and called the whole process the Greek miracle.

If the beginnings are obscure, the rest of the process is sufficiently clear for our purpose. Athenian achievements in the direction of free discussion were part of a general trend toward popular male autonomy that culminated in democracy. In Athens there is hardly any sign that public policy was ever set by an all-powerful divine monarch. Even though the notion of impiety remained strong, one can hardly speak of religion as setting the framework for politics in historical times. Instead the trend was toward men getting together in small or large gatherings to argue out with each other what they ought to do. That of course is the essence of rational discussion. It is unlikely that the Athenians or any other Greeks invented this version of rational discussion because it occurs widely in nonliterate societies. Nevertheless this was the first attempt to make it work in a "civilized" society, that is, one with a written language.

The politics of the ancient theocratic monarchies and of classical civilization itself were violent. This violence, and the high-level of political tension behind it, imposed a severe strain on rational discussion. In classical Greece two issues dominated the politics of the day: one domestic and the other foreign. The two were related and sometimes coalesced. The domestic issue was whether the "many," or the "poor," or, as we might say, "the masses" would take away the property of the well-to-do and physically destroy them. Likewise there were the issues of whether one city-state would take over another one and how the wealthy and the poor in each of the contesting states would line up in relation to each other. With this continually high level of conflict it is hardly surprising that the controls over political partisanship were weak and debates often venomous.

From this review two propositions emerge: (1) Popular sovereignty, or at least movement in that direction, is essential to rational discussion. Without popular sovereignty, rational discussion becomes meaningless. We will reserve for later the question of whether rational discussion is necessarily an elitist practice *within* a system of popular sovereignty. (2) A high level of political tension, especially conflicts that threaten the existence of important segments in the societies of a given political system, creates great difficulties for rational discussion. There is probably a point at which such discussion becomes impossible or is stopped by sheer physical force. Again the time and situation of this crisis may vary considerably in accord with a society's historically determined political culture.

Chinese society presents an instructive contrast that supports the generalizations suggested by ancient Athens. In China there were some important factors, mainly intellectual traditions, favoring the development of rational discussion. These had appeared in predynastic times. As pointed out above, Mencius had stressed the obligations of the ruler to his people and the right and obligation to criticize an unjust ruler. In sharp contrast to Athens the "gentlemanly" ethos of Confucianism was very much opposed to vehement partisanship.

But rational discussion could play no more than a limited role under the single authority of an emperor, who could, at least in the short run, reject any advice presented to him. Beyond limited and shifting personal factions among the higher officials, there was no effective organized pressure group behind alternative policies. As a memorandum culture instead of an oral and rhetorical one like Athens, there were limited opportunities for rational discussion. The only audience that mattered was the emperor himself. "Good" emperors were overloaded with reports, while "bad" ones paid no attention.

With the advantages of hindsight we may also see that certain ingredients for a working system of rational discussion were absent in both classical Athens and early China. Oratory is not really discussion. There is no give and take during a powerful speech. Formal debate before a large audience is only a little better. Both are really attempts to sway the masses. A memorandum partakes even less of the character of a discussion. It is a private statement whose effect is often unknown to the author. Contrary views are also likely to be unknown. In other words there was as yet in these two different early societies no really suitable social framework for rational discussion. That is true even though the potential was present in the Athenian law courts and in Chinese imperial guarantees of freedom of criticism by scholar-officials, guarantees which were often violated. Free discussion is a delicate plant. It needs an institutional setting where it can grow protected against the arbitrary commands and demands of a ruler as well as against the gusts of passion from an outraged crowd. In this sense of requiring a buffer against the outside world, free discussion is an elite institution. The need for special training in logical exposition and the restraint of partisanship reinforces this elite character. No wonder the man in the street or behind the plow, as well as his hard-pressed spouse, have been suspicious of and hostile toward this form of rationality.

IV

At this point we may continue our historical soundings by turning to later western history for information about forces favoring and opposing the practice of rational discussion. The most obvious opposition came from organized Christianity, or more precisely the Catholic Church. This is not the place to recite the Church's often bloody attempts to suppress heresy. It is obvious enough that a mentality that seeks out heresy and tries to destroy heretics is, to say the least, unfavorable to rational discussion. Heresy hunting was a scourge and a form of cruelty unknown to classical civilization, though the seeds of such behavior are plain enough in the treatment of the inhabitants of Canaan by the ancient Hebrews. It is nearly impossible to have a real discussion when some participants hold that other participants' beliefs are dangerously evil. In medieval Western Europe the first impulse toward toleration may have come from commercial contacts in the cosmopolitan port cities, especially those of the Low Countries. After all, the important things about a merchant were the goods he brought to sell, their quality, and the prices he wanted. Fellow traders were not really interested in the religion he professed. In this situation religion was, so to speak, bracketed and its salience greatly reduced. This appears to be the fundamental social and psychological mechanism behind the rise of toleration. However the impulse from the medieval port cities was not strong enough to carry the process very far. The bloodiest struggles were yet to come in the wars of religion, from 1559 to 1648.

These wars began as straightforward religious conflicts, as the Catholic Church, with considerable success, tried to regain territories lost to Protestantism. Later other interests came to the fore, most noticeably those of the emerging national state. The downgrading of religion was more important in this context and contributed more to de facto toleration than events in the port cities. After the fighting had gone on for decades it seemed to many thoughtful men to have reached a stand off. More fighting could only mean more killing—and for what? Furthermore acute rulers and their advisers began to see that they could gain more through strengthening their own state by stiffening and extending royal bureaucracies, by improving their armies, and thereby earning a better place in the system of alliances, than they could by pouring out blood and treasure in pursuit of the triumph of "true" religion. Thus the significance of religion lost ground to the interests of the national state. This weakening of the demand for religious conformity favored the prospects for rational discussion.

There was a time, say, shortly before the First World War, when one could end the story there on a note of decisive victory over the forces of obscurantism. That is no longer possible. Two closely related considerations destroy this rationalistic optimism. In the first place we have to notice that the downgrading of the religious obstacle to free discussion takes place only through the substitution of another overriding value. In the case of the port cities it was money. In the case of the religious wars it was the new national state. Both money and the state readily become dominant values and destructive goals in their own right. In the twentieth century, and even before, both became idols beyond criticism. They have also been a source of bloodshed, intensified by modern technology, that greatly exceeds the slaughter of the wars of religion.

From the standpoint of finding and encouraging the social and psychological prerequisites of rational discussion under contemporary conditions, we can see more clearly how severe the obstacles are. As just suggested, the issues of the day cannot carry so high an emotional charge that compromise and dispassionate rational discussion become impossible. Yet reducing the emotional charge can be difficult because local grassroots leaders spend a great deal of energy trying to raise the emotional salience of the issues in order to retain or increase their following. This process is especially visible in the history of ethnic minorities, labor movements, and religious minorities.

In the case of movements of political and religious mobilization, such as communism, fascism, and certain forms of Christianity, we can observe a reduction of the emotional charge inherent in the official doctrines after the movement has held power for at least a dozen years. By this time the movement may have already done enormous damage, far more than just the destruction of institutions connected with rational discussion. In an aging religious and political movement the most noticeable features are disappointment at the movement's failure to achieve frequently promised goals, and boredom with a propaganda that continues to urge discipline on behalf of these goals. This propaganda ceases to make sense in terms of the ordinary citizen's daily experience. That may be the case for quite some years without producing an obvious loss of faith. But if signs appear that a segment of the top leadership has also lost faith, and for that reason punishment for failure to go through the rituals of allegiance is no longer swift, sure, and dependable, overt loss of faith can spread with astonishing speed. Parallel with this loss of faith there is a turn toward hedonism, at least among those who can afford it. If the future no longer seems attainable or worth struggling for, why not enjoy the present as best one can?

These transformations of the official faith are visible in the USSR and somewhat less obviously so in China. Similar cultural trends appeared in Christian Europe during the Renaissance prior to the Counter-Reformation. Disenchantment, boredom, and increasing hedonism quite clearly reduce the emotional charge of ideals and symbols that have moved men's hearts.

On the other hand, can disenchantment, boredom, and hedonism provide adequate emotional nourishment for the growth of rational discussion? The answer seems doubtful. For rational discussion to take root, there has to be some sense of a social order worth working for, a sober awareness that this is not going to happen without serious dispute and some confidence in the role of rational discussion in settling these disputes. All this is tragically missing from the experience of both the USSR and China.

From the foregoing discussion one could gain the impression that any form of strongly held beliefs, religious or secular, about moral and immoral forms of human behavior would have consequences unfavorable for rational discussion. If some kinds of human behavior are deemed to be absolutely evil, there is no use discussing the matter, not even the causes of such behavior. True believers are not much interested in causes because the causes of evil seem so obvious. Believers want to extirpate an evil before the rot spreads. That is why we hear so much about "cleaning out" and "purification"—usually with strong punitive overtones—not only in Stalinist and Nazi propaganda, but also in portions of the Old Testament.

All this is true. But there is also good evidence to show that the link between intense transcendental belief and hostility to rational discussion is not universal and requires careful specification. In 1932 Rufus M. Jones published the influential study of mystic sectarianism and its contribution to democracy, *Mysticism and Democracy in the English Commonwealth*. The central idea of much of this mysticism, especially the later phase in the seventeenth century, was in Jones's words "a glowing faith that there is something divine in man, which under right influences and responses can become the dominant feature of a person's whole life" (p. 121). Clearly the English mystics were as passionately religious as human beings can become. It is also clear that a religion stressing a belief in the spark of divinity in all men (and women too in some cases, it seems), is not likely to develop into an oppressive system of religious conformity. There was too great a respect for the individual conscience for that to happen. Most of the mystics (but not all—the Familists were an exception[see p. 129]) developed democratic forms of organization for their religious communities. In these communities there was much discussion of moral and religious issues by ordinary rank and file members. Such discussion was both practice in and practice for democracy.

To sum up, religious passion need not always have obscurantist consequences. If this passion has a democratic or perhaps even populist turn, mainly a belief in the worth of the individual, it may under favorable circumstances, especially when granted some toleration by a higher authority, impart an impulse toward free and rational discussion. It is when this passion, in either a religious or secular form, stresses an exclusive possession of truth and morality, that there appears an ominous threat to freedom and rationality. Since new and passionate beliefs are most likely to appear in a period of social disorder and severe conflict, a democratic outcome seems rare and improbable.

There is one further reason for the frequency of a destructive outcome. In itself the ideal of rational discussion is not very exciting. It also carries elitist overtones of well-educated and well-to-do men sitting in a comfortably appointed and tastefully paneled board room discussing the miseries of ordinary people, miseries they have never experienced directly and never will. Hence in times of political or religious excitement the ideal of rational discussion can scarcely get a hearing. It is drowned out by the cries of "*à la lanterne!*" When the excitement dies down, people may or may not realize that they have been ruled from board rooms all along, even at the height of the excitement. To be sure, the people in the board rooms may have been somewhat different, and the physical appointments for a time less imposing, but whether the excitement led to more rational discussions in the revolutionary board rooms is another question. The answer appears to be negative. Rational discussion is often boring and requires a long period of boring politics with unexciting issues to get established.

V

By way of conclusion let us try to set down the major factors favorable and unfavorable to the development of rational discussion. It seems harder to point to favorable factors than unfavorable ones, a difficulty that may be significant. Nevertheless it will be well to begin with favorable or at least facilitating conditions.

One that seems to me crucial, though I do not recollect any discussion of it in the literature, is the development of generally accepted rules of logic and standards of evidence to guide and control disputes. On this score Western civilization owes a major debt to classical Greece.

The establishment of such standards is no easy task. Still such an intellectual achievement does not have to be anywhere near complete in order to be helpful. It is not necessary that everybody be a trained logician before taking part in a serious discussion about politics or anything else. Even a dim awareness that there are objective restraints on what one can say and still make sense helps to check irresponsible assertions and accusations. If one thinks of Hitler as a counterexample, one has to remember that the Nazis never won a majority in a free election.

Standards of argument seem most secure in those intellectual fields most remote from the study of human passions and concerns, namely mathematics and the physical sciences. Yet even in these subjects we have noticed acrimonious debate over fundamentals. There appears to be rather less passionate investment in a particular intellectual position when the concern is concrete research. A natural scientist, and for that matter a social scientist, who tries to "find out something about something" can count on a fairly high degree of rational discussion of the methods used and findings proposed.

As we turn from general scientific and scholarly discussion to rational discussion of political issues, it is reasonably clear that an educated elite able to participate actively in political affairs is a minimum requirement for the existence of rational political debate. Whether the debate can remain rational if the participants extend much beyond the elite is an issue much discussed at present.

Two observations are pertinent. Confining political debate to an educated elite is no guarantee by itself that discussion will be rational. The elite's education may be unsuitable and its general temper too arrogant for serious discussion of political matters. As for the rest of the population, the same considerations apply. They may or may not, depending on historical factors, have the knowledge and temperament suitable for any form of rational discussion, of which the political one is the most difficult.

The discussion so far has been about people who actually engage in rational discussion or at least try to. They have usually been a minority. A few words are necessary about the social atmosphere in which the rest of the population lives. Rather obviously it has to be an atmosphere of economic and political security. Concretely, that means there is no very serious threat to life and property from within the society or from foreign sources. Obviously this is a relatively rare situation in human history. And it is beginning to look as though rational discussion is likely to flourish most where it is least needed: where political passions are minimal. On that discouraging note we may end the discussion of favorable factors.

The factors unfavorable to the practice of rational discussion seem easier to identify than those just discussed. They include a high-level of political excitement, an authoritarian (and later totalitarian) regime that tolerates little or no opposition, a powerless educated elite, and—most dangerous of all—a religious or quasireligious belief in the way human society ought to be organized, or will be organized. In the twentieth century such beliefs have included a racially pure warrior society and a classless society.

This collection of factors, I suggest, boils down to the creation of extreme partisanship or, more precisely, fright at the prospect of what could happen to cherished hopes and beliefs under dispassionate critical examination. Beneath bluster and the endless reassertion of doctrinal orthodoxy (which can change every twenty-four hours in totalitarian regimes) there is, I think, a fear lest the justification for one's existence could crumble away if exposed to the light of rational inquiry.

It would be a serious mistake to leave the impression that the habit of rational discussion will appear and grow where conditions are favorable and the obstacles not very severe. The process is by no means so automatic. Some concrete and strategically placed individuals have to get an ideal before a new idea can take hold in any culture. There is no way to guarantee that there will be such individuals or that the new ideal can be transformed into new social habits.

Yet, when it does appear, rational discussion is one of the finest flowers of human civilization. It is the embodiment of intelligence, restraint, civility, and cultivation.

What Is Not Worth Knowing

In this essay I shall explore the idea that there are many things an intelligent and educated person should not know. To put the point in a slightly different way, I shall argue that there is such a thing as intellectual and even emotional trash, and that it is harmful to stuff the human head with too much of it. But how can we identify it? More specifically, when we call some piece of information pure trash, how can we be sure that we are doing anything more than expressing some kind of snobbish prejudice? Today one person's trash looks like a neglected masterpiece to someone else. From a relativist standpoint there can be no such thing as worthless knowledge. But no serious thinker works without *some* criteria for sifting knowledge. In order to get a better grasp on our problem let us see how the sifting usually works.

Most professionals have to be uninformed about huge blocks of knowledge outside their area of special competence. Such a decision to avoid the acquisition of knowledge does not however, carry any implication that other forms of knowledge are not worth having. A physicist's decision not to learn the economic history of Japan from 1867 to 1900 does not automatically imply that this history is not worth knowing. Professional thinkers as a group may make thousands of decisions a day that result in voluntarily assumed ignorance. These are matters of intellectual economy, concessions, if you will, to human frailty and the biological impossibility of omniscience.

These decisions are not what we are looking for. Indeed, rather the opposite. We are trying to find out if there are kinds of knowledge that are intrinsically trivial or worthless even though they can be exciting and attractive as entertainment for many people. A century ago hardly any serious thinker would have bothered with such a question because the answer seemed too obvious, even though the reasoning behind similar

Delivered as the Walter Edge Lecture, Princeton, April 12, 1989.

answers was quite varied. There were those who felt that worthwhile knowledge was different from vulgar knowledge and trash, and that anyone who could not grasp the difference right off was not worth talking to anyway. Then there were the Marxists who believed that all "real" problems appeared on the historical agenda at the same time that solutions to them became available. Capitalism was a solution to one set of problems and socialism the answer to the next set. Any work on intellectual issues not obviously part of the historical agenda was for the Marxist simply an evasion. In this instance an evasion meant trash or something very close to trash. Often enough, the Marxist conception of intellectual trash becomes a form of self-protecting dogma. That is one damaging feature of the Marxist conception. Another is the lack of any room for an aesthetic criterion. Marxism is heavy-footed in its utilitarian emphasis. Nevertheless, the Marxist emphasis on the changing historical component in the meaning of significance and importance has been a valuable intellectual contribution.

Finally there is the liberal tradition. Where uncontaminated by traditional elitism or Marxism, the liberal tradition advocates a democracy of curiosity. One question, one issue is just as good as any other question or issue. There is no way to decide which is more important among them. Kinship in an exotic nonliterate tribe stands on the same level of importance as the connection between German big business and the Nazis at the end of the Weimar Republic.

This democratic liberalism in the search for truth was appropriate to England, the classic land of the cultivated amateur who chose his own topic and ways of pursuing it. Discussion with other amateurs provided the sanctions that validated the findings in accord with generally accepted rules of logic. Democratic liberalism has also survived in American and British universities where it justifies teaching just about anything and everything a professor wants to teach or investigate. There is an informal but very strong taboo on raising questions about the significance of a colleague's work. If the colleague thinks it is important and the funds and students are available, that is enough.

To be sure there are those who are quite aware that democracy of curiosity cannot possibly serve as a rationale for allocating scarce intellectual and material resources among competing tasks and projects. For instance, the instructions that accompany requests from the National Endowment for the Humanities for assessments of scholarly projects acknowledge bluntly that not every project is equally significant. But like others faced with the same general issue, they refrain, perhaps wisely, from telling us what makes the difference. To state the criteria openly would intensify existing quarrels and provoke new ones.

Obviously it is not just the talent of the individual scientist or scholar that makes the difference, important though this quality may be. To stress the importance of the individual investigator merely pushes the question one step backward up the causal chain. What is it about the investigator that leads one to recognize superiority? The superior investigator is one who recognizes that not all facts (or questions about facts) are equally significant. By now that has begun to seem obvious. The notion of a democracy of curiosity just won't wash. It is neither a description of what happens nor a serviceable prescription of what ought to happen in any form of serious intellectual inquiry. But if not all questions and not all answers are equal, what makes them different?

To ask this question is to ask, What are the criteria for evaluating knowledge? I suggest that there are essentially two criteria: a utilitarian criterion and an aesthetic one. They are visible, I believe, behind all the variations over time and space that appear in the record of human curiosity. The utilitarian or instrumental criterion comes in three shapes, possibly more. The acquisition of knowledge that diminishes human suffering, as in the case of medicine for the most part, certainly satisfies the utilitarian criterion. By any standard it is useful knowledge. But so also is destructive knowledge that increases human suffering. Military technology is the most obvious example. In this connection it is necessary to emphasize that we are discussing here the ways human societies actually have evaluated the search for knowledge and are likely to do so over the foreseeable future, not the way they ought to evaluate knowledge according to an ethical ideal.

There is one more possible form of the utilitarian criterion. Any form of knowledge that contributes or promises to contribute to human happiness might meet the utilitarian criterion. Here, however, we run into serious difficulty. It is almost impossible to assess any given piece of knowledge in terms of its effect on human happiness, because there are so many forms and levels of human happiness — such as the excitement one may feel from coordinating muscles and brain in work or play, to minimal satisfaction on receiving a birthday card from a barely welcome well-wisher. Even the debate about ethically desirable forms of happiness continually changes. Both the effect and the happiness are too protean to yield worthwhile judgments. To talk about the importance (or acceptability) of human knowledge in terms of its contribution to human happiness lands us back in the quagmire of a democracy of curiosity out of which we have just tried to crawl.

One way to cope with this problem might be to work out a rough scale of forms of social happiness as opposed to merely individual pleasure. Then one might be able to assess the importance of one piece of knowledge—or the search for such knowledge—in terms of its contribution to social happiness. Actually we make similar estimates quite often anyway, without going through all the logical steps such a judgment requires. But there are serious dangers down this road. Who is to determine what social happiness means and on what basis? Twentieth-century dictators have given far from reassuring answers. In such a dictatorship social happiness is what the dictator tells the population it ought to feel. Social happiness can become an instrument of arbitrary and terrorist rule, like the notion of virtue at the height of the French Revolution. "Social happiness" suggests group compulsion to be happy, directed at individuals who want to drown out their own unhappiness. The whole notion evokes the sound of a male chorus singing "healthy" songs against the flickering light of a bonfire, a scene full of camaraderie and community, with strong young men tossing books into the fire.

The best way to deal with this set of confusions and ambiguities, I still think, is to ignore it by dropping the whole issue of happiness and sticking to the reduction of the more extreme forms of human misery as the main utilitarian criterion for judging knowledge and assessing the search for new knowledge. There is enough extreme poverty, disease, and cruelty in the world to keep professional thinkers busy for a long time to come. In saying this I do not wish to imply that all serious inquiry has to be about social pathologies past and present. Such an attitude would lead to a sour-faced earnestness, not to significant truth. To understand these pathologies we have to know how human societies work and how human nature behaves under more "normal" or less stressful conditions. What little knowledge we have of this kind is precious, and we need a great deal more.

Let us move on then to the aesthetic criterion for assessing the importance of one or more truths. Its essence is the discovery of order and pattern in the universe or parts of it. For a long time astronomy was the classic example of aesthetically ordered inquiry, though there arose an instrumental element through its contribution to navigation. Many forms of knowledge mix utilitarian and aesthetic components, even though the two are analytically distinct. Later, physics and chemistry took over from astronomy as sciences with a powerful aesthetic component. Pure math-ematics has of course all along been the science of possible forms of order. It has often been remarked that the social sciences have not been able to achieve the degree of logical rigor and aesthetically attractive patterning found in mathematics and the natural sciences. When the social sciences try to follow the model of the natural sciences too closely, they are liable to turn into grotesque parodies. They can become pseudosciences sus-tained by pseudofacts, a creation easy to market among military intelli-gence officers and, in business, marketing and investment advisers.

By no means do all aesthetically pleasing patterns turn up in the natural sciences. Scientists prefer relatively simple "classical" patterns and are in-clined to avoid "gothic" or "romantic" exuberance. The scientists' aim is to account for as large a number of facts with as simple a set of propo-sitions as possible. A large number of social scientists share this aim, and even historians on occasion have found it attractive despite their quite justifiable emphasis on the particular and the unique. Recent develop-ments in physics have, on the other hand, pushed researchers toward a much more willing acceptance of highly complex and "romantic" patterns. These developments have been taking place in a set of problems loosely and somewhat misleadingly labeled the study of chaos. So far as this out-sider can make out, these scientists and mathematicians search for patterns and order in phenomena like turbulence in the flow of gases and liquids, where chaos apparently prevails and no ordering principle seems apparent. They have by and large succeeded. But the order in chaos often turns out to be bizarre and complex in comparison to other known forms of order. Often it is also very beautiful. Conceivably this research may lead to far-reaching changes in scientific conceptions of pattern and order. But it is too early to tell now.

Discussion of the aesthetic criterion for distinguishing what is worth knowing from what is not leads to the question of whether similar criteria may apply to the emotions. At first glance the answer appears negative. Knowledge takes the form of assertions about facts. The assertions may be true or false with a number of degrees of uncertainty in between. The emotions, on the other hand, have to do with feelings. As such, feelings have nothing to do with truth or falsehood. They are just there as part of the human reaction to experience.

But is the distinction between knowledge and emotion as sharp as all that? To a great extent human emotional responses are learned responses. The emotional repertoire of a five-year-old child is only a fraction of the repertoire of a thirty-five-year-old adult. Emotion shares with knowledge a learned component: the individual has to learn how to feel and express emotions, even though feelings, unlike factual knowledge, almost certainly have an ultimate biological source. Among highly educated people literature, art, and music make a major contribution to emotional learning. It is a vicarious form of learning in which young people learn and even experience feelings by familiarizing themselves with the reported sensations of literary and artistic models. In social groups and cultures with less of a formal educational system, emotional learning takes place by listening to and questioning the tales of the older generation and near contemporaries. There is also a great deal of simple observation about how grown-ups feel and behave in different situations. In this fashion one learns at the very least whom to hate, what to fear, and whom to love.

Human beings are not born with these responses, at least not with specific targets for the release of emotional discharges. From one person to another there is also much variation. Quite a number of individuals seem incapable of emotional reactions, as any teacher will testify. For large numbers of young people in our society it is especially difficult to step outside the confines of their own local culture and empathize with the suffering or joys of a literary or historical figure from another time or place. To the young this kind of empathy may seem just silly. With advancing age and declining understanding such empathy for "foreign" ways is liable to appear threatening. The reaction will then be a taut-lipped and even vicious xenophobia.

These considerations indicate that there are feelings not worth having (leaving aside the morally reprehensible ones) just as there are facts not worth knowing. They are trash insofar they fail to meet the utilitarian and aesthetic criteria. Both forms of trash are traceable to educational failures. In the case of emotions there are grounds for criticizing those who display some kinds of emotions as well as those incapable of certain types of emotional response. Misdirected hostility is an example of the first and an incapacity for human sympathy or affection is an example of the second. The parallel with facts one should and should not know appears reasonably clear. Nevertheless it is far from easy to find our way to the next step and specify clearly what kinds of emotions are not worth having. Many intelligent people, to be sure, sound as though there were no problem here. From time to time we hear criticism of trashy, cheap, and trivial emotions. But are these adjectives anything more than a string of snobbish epithets? Or do they refer to an identifiable way of feeling and behaving?

It may be possible to identify this emotional pattern by taking an indirect route through criticisms of popular taste and the emotions associated therewith as well as efforts to distinguish genuine art from entertainment. Admittedly this route presents certain dangers. Lambasting popular taste has been an indoor sport for discontented intellectuals with and without artistic gifts ever since the days of Flaubert, if not Plato. There is an odor of partisan apologetics about these claims. Yet behind the pyrotechnics we may come upon important social and psychological facts.

We can begin with two widely accepted characteristics of what we can call genuine art and the kind of emotional reactions expected from it. First, genuine art has a high degree of coherence and form, or at the very least an intuitively recognizable style. In the second place — and for the purpose at hand this is more important — genuine art puts before us a recurring human dilemma such as unrequited love, the impact of death, or the conflict of deeply felt obligations. The dilemma is often one for which no solution is possible, at least not in the historical epoch during which the work of art is created. To give some examples, even to an untrained ear Beethoven's music clearly has form and style despite all the sudden loud emphatic phrases and romantic flourishes. Tolstoy's treatment of the social and psychological impact of death in *The Death of Ivan Ilich* and of conflicting emotional demands and obligations in *Anna Karenina* are both acknowledged masterpieces. But because there is much less guilt associated with adultery nowadays, the story of Anna Karenina has probably lost much of its force. The dilemma is not so insoluble as it seemed in the nineteenth century. Nevertheless, unfaithfulness remains a highly charged emotional situation despite all the air of sophisticated tolerance. Thus in the case of really great art, and the emotions it is expected to create, we can still say of the person who is not moved: there is something wrong with the person, not with the art. The observation also applies to the individual who has no response to the great works of non-Western cultures.

It is the other way around, I suggest, with the trashy entertainments and shallow emotions whose characteristics I shall now try to specify. There is something wrong with a person whose emotions stir only in response to such stimuli or who devotes too much time to them. There are good reasons for suspecting that such a person never had the opportunity or the desire to grow up. In other words, the love of trash may be a phase in the emotional growth of the individual, at least in modern Western society. On a worldwide scale, however, it scarcely looks like a transient phase. Socialist societies have an insatiable appetite for adolescent capitalist trash.

In comparison with the music of Mozart and Beethoven, in my opinion, contemporary popular music lacks real form. Instead it usually displays simple very repetitive themes over a monotonous beat. The emotions it tries to arouse are easily accessible: an eroticized gaiety or more often an eroticized self-pity and sadness. Where great art manages to depict a typical situation without turning it into a cardboard sociological category, modern trash appeals to self-centered sentimentality, as if one's disappointment were the only one in the world that mattered. Popular entertainments rarely present permanent human problems that have no solution. Instead they choose reassuring familiar subjects and settings. The settings tend to be pseudorealistic, that is, sanitized; disagreeable elements are reduced to jokes we can all supposedly share. (Thus, we find pseudoexotic settings, such as the tropics without bugs.) In this way modern media promote a passive and rather shallow escapism. The emotional problems that the media present are by and large banal in at least two senses. Since so little of ordinary daily behavior remains subject to taboo, especially in "trend-setting" circles, a great deal of human behavior becomes banal. Even sex loses its emotional charge as it turns into one more form of recreation. The problems are banal for a further reason: anyone with a minimal supply of common sense can see a solution. The woman who fails to realize that the man with whom she has been living for two years has no intention of marrying her may be an object of some pity. But not much. The element of self-deception reduces our sympathy.

To be sure, trashy emotions may be intense and quite painful for a brief period of time. But they are ephemeral and can be forgotten, especially if replaced by a new stimulus. For that matter the emotion may remain pretty much the same while the person requires a new stimulus at frequent short intervals to generate the sensation of being a human being. Is that perhaps the reason why radios keep on blaring fourth-rate jazz as youngsters try to study and house painters try to paint? Or does this disagreeable and inconsiderate habit reflect a fear of being left alone with one's thoughts? Whatever the reason, trash goes into the human head and spirit whenever this happens.

It is important to recognize that trashy and trivial information often exerts far greater attraction than valuable knowledge just as the appeal of cheap and shallow emotions easily outweighs deeper and more discriminating ones. There are a variety of reasons for the triumph of triviality.

The mere fact that much of it is already labeled as entertainment means that there is no reason to take it seriously. There is no need for strain and effort. (By this observation I do not imply that forms that require strain and effort are therefore good. Often they are just fake.) Indeed the main point of entertainment *is* distraction from real and serious problems, intellectual or emotional. Trivial entertainment often mimics serious problems in real life, insofar as it centers on aggression and strategy—but in a way that extracts most of the bite and poison. Amateur chess, checkers, and poker are examples.

Collecting miscellaneous and essentially trivial objects such as stamps is another widespread form of recreation, especially in the United States. The role of aggression seems to be less in such activities, though rivalry certainly exists. Collecting appears to be mainly a way of creating little islands of personally controlled order in a chaotic and threatening world. There is also the pleasure of recognizing or completing a pattern. Completing a pattern is generally easier in adding to a collection of say, mediocre Victorian glassware, than in sorting out the essentials of complicated business deals and legal arrangements in real life. And, finally, does not the avid collector have the right to ask, "Which is the real life anyway? That where the money comes from or that where the money gives pleasure?" To reply that the question reflects a pathetic and impoverished hedonism will hardly satisfy the questioner.

Before coming to a close I want to make a few remarks to avoid possible misunderstandings and perhaps smooth out unnecessarily ruffled feathers. I am not making an argument for some bureaucratic authority to determine the prospective worth of every piece of scholarly research and scientific investigation. There is enough of that around already. When the bureaucracy becomes omnipotent and serves a single overriding doctrine, as was the case in Stalinist Russia and only somewhat less so in Nazi Germany as well as in wartime Japan, the consequences are disastrous not only for scholars and scientists but also for the general population. At the same time it is necessary to recognize that there cannot be any such thing as complete intellectual autonomy—or for that matter complete emotional autonomy. No matter how much some scientists and scholars may work alone, a practice that varies greatly from one field to another, they are dependent on the larger society for the support of their activities. They also depend on both the larger society and each other for judgment about the worth of their work. The selection of issues for investigation depends greatly upon career prospects and pressure from colleagues. Beneath these social determinants one can discern a bedrock of objective reality. Issues and problems are there whether anybody sees them or not. They change historically as do the intellectual tools available to cope with them.

Insofar as complete intellectual autonomy is a pipe dream, scholars and scientists have to work out and apply criteria for evaluating their products themselves or have it done for them and done badly. A great deal of this evaluation takes place in a somewhat haphazard way anyhow. I have tried to suggest how the arguments might become more explicit, comprehensible, and where mistaken, subject to reasoned correction. The best we can probably hope for in the way of an institutional setting is, to paraphrase a familiar quip about the Hapsburg Empire, a bureaucracy softened by sloppiness, wealth, and intellectual curiosity. That situation provides a reasonable prospect for intellectual diversity, innovation, and growth. The other prospects are much less pleasant to contemplate. One is a comb-out and *Gleichschaltung* of university life in the manner of Margaret Thatcher. In the United States the yahoos and other vindictive antiintellectuals might gain control of the process. Another possibility, and perhaps a more likely one, is a generalized refusal of professional thinkers to discuss the rationale of their work out of a *pudeur des sentiments* and a fear of upsetting collegial arrangements. That road can only lead us further down toward the fragmentation and disintegration of Western culture, a process threatening enough in its own right. But the reactionary redeemers that crop up along the way are liable to be much worse.

Finally I do not seek to present here a thinly disguised neo-Puritan argument against all forms of emotional release through distraction and entertainment. Life would be even harder to bear without an occasional easy pleasure. On the other hand, I remain suspicious of anyone with an esoteric academic specialty who displays detailed knowledge of television dramas and not much else. That is intellectual snobbishness in reverse. A person whose main pleasures are limited to mass-produced entertainment and distraction is culturally impoverished to the point of being damaged goods intellectually and emotionally. An individual who is unable to distinguish between trivial and significant forms of knowledge, or cheap transient emotions and deep mature feelings, will soon get a head and a heart that look like the inside of an unemptied vacuum cleaner. If the machine doesn't blow a fuse, it will only work at about one quarter of its capacity, and usually with unbearable screeching noises.

"Bequests of the Twentieth Century to the Twenty-first" In Memory of William Graham Sumner

William Graham Sumner was my intellectual grandfather—first in the somewhat personal sense that I was a graduate student of Sumner's junior colleague and collaborator, Albert Galloway Keller. In the second and more important sense, Sumner was my intellectual grandfather inasmuch as I soaked myself in his writings, reading and rereading *Folkways* and his *Essays* (edited by Albert Galloway Keller and Maurice R. Davie, 2 vols. [New Haven, 1934]). Among the *Essays* is one with the title "The Bequests of the Nineteenth Century to the Twentieth." The essay was written in 1901 and later revised. But at that time it was not published. Its first public appearance seems to have been in the *Yale Review* 22 (Summer 1933), 732–754. As prophecy Sumner's essay is not very impressive. He has nothing to say about two world wars or the rise and failure of fascism and communism. But the term "bequests" does not imply specific prophecies, though it may have overtones suggesting them. Strictly speaking "bequests" meant for Sumner the economic, political, and other trends which the nineteenth century bequeathed to the twentieth, and with which the twentieth century would have to come to terms. On that score Sumner's essay turns in a superior performance. One of Sumner's most attractive traits was that his speeches and writings were completely free of the high-minded and edifying themes audiences still expect on ritual occasions. Thus his essay stresses the sources of severe conflict bequeathed to the twentieth century by the nineteenth. No nonsense about democracy and brotherly love in Sumner!

Recalling Sumner's "Bequests of the Nineteenth Century to the Twentieth" a short time ago I concluded that a similar effort by his intellectual grandchild roughly a century later might deserve more than an indulgent smile. That is really up to the reader to decide. The most to be claimed in advance is that truth can arise from obvious error. Furthermore at my age the possibility of learning the results of a reality test of the theses about to be presented below is comfortably close to zero. Thus the present author is reasonably well shielded from the normal sanctions against error and unsound opinions, namely the delight of one's colleagues. Were the situation otherwise this little inquiry might never have taken written form.

Let us begin with two major social conflicts that have given the twentieth century its distinctive character but are unlikely to be important in the twenty-first. One of these is war on the scale of the two world wars. The other is revolution on the scale of the Russian and Chinese revolutions.

From the standpoint of this inquiry the important aspect of the twentieth century's big wars is that sooner or later all major powers, as well as some minor ones, became combatants. This happened mainly because those who did the most toward starting the war were the ones defeated in the end. In starting the war they had some idea they could win it. The distribution of power in the international arena in 1914 and 1939 was not so unequal as to make the prospect of victory for the Central Powers and the Axis Powers look like an utter pipe dream.

Well before the end of the twentieth century the disintegration of the Soviet Union ended the possibility of any roughly equal coalitions among the great powers. In fact there weren't any great powers any more in the sense of states with "vital" interests all over the globe. There was only one: The United States. Its rule could be, has been, and probably will be challenged locally with firepower and casualties. Yet the possibility of putting together a coalition sufficiently powerful to attack and humble the United States is for the time being quite remote. There is probably enough free floating hostility to the United States and its ways in the economically backward areas of the world to make such a coalition at least thinkable. But the loose cannons given to preying on such situations do not yet have enough powder to make them threatening.

In the longer run the prospect of wars that are more than local becomes much more serious. American hegemony is not and cannot be permanent. Power once possessed, can be dangerous to lose, as Thucydides has Pericles say to his Athenian critics: "for by this time the empire you hold is a tyranny, which it may seem wrong to grasp, but dangerous to let go."

(*History of the Peloponnesian War*, 2.63, 2–3). Beyond this level of generality it is unprofitable to inquire here.

Now that we have seen some reasons why another world war appears unlikely in the foreseeable future we may examine the reasons for holding that another revolution with worldwide reverberation is also improbable. First it is necessary to grasp the historical character, limitations, and achievements of past revolutions, at least in major outline. The great revolutionary wave began with the Revolt of the Netherlands in the sixteenth century. It continued with the Puritan Revolution in England and the execution of King Charles I. The next major wave was the French Revolution followed by the American Civil War, and finally in the twentieth century the Bolshevik Revolution in Russia and its offshoot the Communist Revolution in China. Each revolution professed general goals of human liberation and accomplished—at large human cost—something toward their achievement: the end of religious and foreign oppression, the abolition of the divine right of kings and the inequities of aristocratic rule, the end of plantation slavery, equality before the law, the possibility of establishing a government by and for free men (and later free women), and the abolition of the scourges of capitalist society (namely, the business cycle and massive unemployment). It is easy to see that these revolutionary objectives form an historical sequence. In that sense, we can speak of a single revolutionary wave from the sixteenth century through the first half of the twentieth. Again from this vantage point it looks as though the great revolutionary wave has run its course to subside into a series of local storms. These can be violent and cause considerable suffering, yet without much noticeable effect on the course of modern civilization. One can see the end of the age of revolutions most clearly by asking one simple question: where in the modern world does a revolution stand a chance of coming to power *and* sending tremors throughout the rest of the world in the manner of the French Revolution and the Bolshevik Revolution? A counter-revolution in the name of supposedly traditional virtues is something else again, to be discussed below.

Three aspects of the intellectual and material situation at the end of the twentieth century are likely to continue well into the twenty-first century and inhibit the rise of any revolutionary movement with pan-human claims. The revelation of the cruelties and coercion in Stalinist Russia and Maoist China has thoroughly discredited the idea of revolution as a tool for human betterment. Professional students of these regimes have known about these horrors for at least a generation and made their findings widely available. As long as the Soviet Union continued to exist, the effect of the findings was limited. It was always possible to remark that one could not make omelets without breaking eggs. With the passage of time, however, it became obvious that the Stalinist regime was not only cruel but incompetent. Its collapse pulled the last supports out from the Leninist intellectual edifice.

Meanwhile the discrediting of Maoism, while no doubt aided by the collapse of Stalinism, has been going on for some time in response to internal Chinese causes. This is not the place to estimate what the outcome will be in the course of the next generation. A mixture of authoritarian politics, central control of the "commanding heights" in the economy, with wide areas open to individual enterprise and carefully controlled freedom to criticize (like Russian self-criticism?) represents one feasible combination. There are of course other combinations, some of which could turn out to be dangerously unworkable. Amid the confusion we can be sure of one thing: any return to the highly coercive pursuit of an egalitarian utopia will remain politically, if not verbally, off limits.

A second aspect of the end of the century scene unfavorable to the rise of large scale revolutionary movements is the absence of any general sense of indignation. There is no worldwide current of thought focused on, say, two or three intolerable abuses. (How abuses become intolerable, and then in time acceptable, would be worth investigating.) Instead indignation currently fragments along lines of ethnic, nationalist, reactionary religious, and antirationalist lines of cleavage. In its day, Marxism presented potential forms of fusion for the world's fragmented indignations. The first one, "Workers of the world unite," fell apart for good when Germany's large disciplined, and ostensibly socialist working class supported the Kaiser's declaration of war. After the First World War the Marxist theory of imperialism was rather more successful in fusing the indignation of the poor and unfortunate in the economically backward parts of the world. The collapse of Stalinism, however, appears to have greatly reduced the confidence and energy behind the idea of imperialism.

Ethnic and religious outrage may seem an unpromising form of anger to any remaining Leninist whose attitude toward Marxist revolutionary doctrine is "Accept no substitutes!! (Except ours!)" One can easily agree that current fashions in indignation hold little promise for a free society in the future. Instead they are a threat. It is a threat that has already included sporadic violence. We already have a counter-revolution under way with diffuse focal points in the Near East and attempts to export the product to the United States. The United States meanwhile is stirring with its home-grown version. It is quite unlikely that any part of the Near

Eastern religious counter-revolution could fuse with or cooperate with its material American counterparts. But if that should happen, American society would face not just a dangerous police problem but a potentially mortal threat.

We may complete the discussion of what is unlikely to take place with some very brief comments on hopes that are widely shared yet unlikely to be realized. One is world peace. There are just too many severe conflicts in the world, a number of which could flare up unexpectedly. They may be local, but they can be vicious and the cause of many deaths and much suffering. Trotsky's formula of "No war, no peace" still covers the probabilities accurately.

Poverty, indeed massive grinding and degrading poverty, is also liable to mark the twenty-first century. In all prosperous countries our unwillingness to do anything about poverty has become increasingly obvious toward the end of the twentieth century. This unwillingness is not explicable in terms of some notion to the effect that the welfare state is too expensive. There is instead a political unwillingness to tap abundant resources, especially those controlled by the military. Behind that unwillingness is a fear of upsetting the prevailing system of privilege and inequality. Fears and hopes on this score have characterized the history of civilization over the past six thousand years. They are not likely to go away after a New Year's party now only a short stretch into the future. There may be a high degree of truth in the claim that there are sufficient resources available to provide a modest living for just about everybody. But the political obstacles to the kind of international and domestic cooperation necessary to generate these resources and distribute them with a touch of equity are, to use an understatement, formidable.

In any attempt to assess the legacies of this century to the next, two issues stand out above the others. One is the plague of AIDS—leaving aside the prospect of old diseases that have become incurable and the discovery of similar new ones. The other is the rise of fundamentalist and antirationalist movements.

For all its horrors, AIDS is the simpler of the two problems, mainly because at present so little useful knowledge about it is available. There is always the possibility that a straightforward medical solution may be discovered in the next few years. Should that happen, the task of getting any remedy, or set of remedies to the people who need them would be daunting at the very least. In the absence of any remedy, there are responsible epidemiologists who estimate that in the near future death from AIDS will make the Black Death seem a puny affair. So horrible will appear the vengeance of the Old Testament's deity against the transgression of sexual prohibitions.

Between these extremes of optimism and pessimism are the painful issues we have with us today, and will have for a long time to come. Even with continued anal intercourse, if people use condoms and stop sharing needles, it appears that prevention is highly effective. Why does not prevention check the plague or cut it back to trivial proportions? Part of the reason must lie in the power of sexual passion to overcome reason. This is not the place to draw the line between a magnificent aspect of our humanity and sheer piggish self-indulgence. Both contribute to AIDS, the latter more so, simply because it leads to more frequent risky sexual acts.

A more important set of considerations comes from the fact that access to and knowledge about prevention are not equally distributed over the world today and have not been so in the past. The situation is not the same in a remote Third World country with a high incidence of AIDS and other diseases as in New York or London. To stress the obvious, AIDS already has a pattern of incidence that is the consequence of this history. It is well known that the incidence is especially heavy among blacks. What statistics there are about this could in the nature of the case hardly be reliable and are certainly liable to rapid change. In any case, for some time to come AIDS is likely to remain unlike the Black Death, a plague with a disproportionately heavy incidence among those at the bottom of the social pyramid. That is one more reason for stressing the observation that AIDS has become a major political problem as well as a medical one. Here the word political can and should have a broad meaning, characterizing the socially organized distribution of misery and happiness in any human society. This distribution is of course the consequence of far more than the workings of political institutions as they are ordinarily perceived and described. Those concerned with and affected by AIDS have long been active. The recent outburst of the black Ethiopian Jews in Israel (*New York Times*, 29 January 1996, p. 1) introduces a distinctly new feature in the tragedy. For the first time, a large group of people—vastly more than just those threatened by the disease—have expressed resentment at being victimized, and have specifically challenged the social distribution of this especially horrible form of human misery. Whether this challenge will amount to anything constructive is almost impossible to determine now. That, in some form, it will be a legacy to the next century does seem sure.

Fundamentalism became a worldwide concern during the last decade of this century. The rise of this concern has been rapid. When I stressed this threat to free institutions in the Tanner lectures at Oxford in 1985, I was dismayed by the total incredulity so politely expressed in a seminar on the lectures. Now before me as I write is a scholarly review of an 852-page book that is the fourth volume in what is known as the Fundamentalism Project, all edited by Martin E. Marty and R. Scott Appleby (See *Contemporary Sociology* 25 [January 1996], 55). This huge academic enterprise with its long list of contributors provides solid evidence for the social acceptance of fundamentalism as a contemporary problem, and an intractable one at that. Once a form of social behavior has passed a threshold and become a problem, one can ordinarily judge the problem's intractability by the number of pages devoted to it and the number of people interested in it.

On inspection I was unable to find more than a few nuggets of useful information, while the rest struck me, quite possibly in error, as either common knowledge available in the *New York Times*, or the work of area specialists with defensive overtones and limited general relevance. If this evaluation seems ungenerous, the passage of time can correct it. Very likely this enormous study will be available a generation or more from now for comparison with reality. That will be the real test. Those who examine these volumes then will have to determine their intellectual shelf life.

Let us now ask what fundamentalist movements want and how they propose to get it. In the first place they create a largely imaginary past of harmony, obedience to legitimate authority, sexual virtue, devotion towards the supernatural, and recognition of the importance of hard work. These are of course the traditional conservative virtues stressed in every major civilization: the Islamic world, Hindu India, Confucian China (*not* the Taoist current, which is one of delightful mockery), and Confucian and Shinto Japan. This fundamentalist view, however, is a caricature of the traditional virtues cobbled together for political purposes. Fundamentalist leaders also display the traits stressed by the great nineteenth-century Swiss historian Jacob Burckhardt's "terrible simplifier." Social remedies are reduced to crude and hostile slogans like "the Jews." The movements display an antirational and anti-intellectual current usually much cruder than presently respectable versions of the same doctrines. They are hostile to foreigners and display a notable inclination toward violence.

Not all of these characteristics appear in all fundamentalist movements. Certainly not with equal emphasis. The really significant one, I suggest, is the use of a glorified past as a blueprint for a utopian future. Even the future may not be all that crucial, in that leaders have no great interest in it. What they are really after are good sticks to beat the present. The emphasis on the political use of the past also brings causal connections to the surface: fundamentalism is most likely to put in an appearance when the conventional virtues are in deep trouble. (They are always in considerable trouble. Otherwise it would not be necessary to take so much trouble inculcating them.) They are in deep trouble when the connection between virtue and its reward becomes more and more difficult to discern.

The emphasis on a "useable past"—ironically, once upon a time, the slogan of left historians—also reveals that decisive elements of fundamentalism have occurred in the past in a way that sheds light on future possibilities. The deservedly famous book by Ronald Syme, *The Roman Revolution* (Oxford, 1939), presents a sardonic picture of Augustus trying to carry out a moral revolution and restore ancient Roman virtues by enlisting Vergil, Horace, and others—hardly public relations hacks—to provide the inspiration. This case, and similar ones to be found in the British and Japanese empires—and for that matter even that of Pericles in the Athenian empire—display important shared features. One could call these features fundamentalism from above—back to basic virtues!— or simple military patriotism. In any case the connection with violence used by and for the state is very plain in fundamentalism from above.

How about fundamentalism from below? It would be easy to catalogue the type of miseries that favor the growth of fundamentalism, such as elderly people who have been left behind in a market economy and are lonely and crave both human companionship and the solace of religion. But it may be more useful to say a few words about a major near contemporary political figure, Mao, because the contradictions in his career are also contradictions in what we are trying to understand. Whether or not he deserves the label fundamentalist is really a secondary matter, though there is considerable evidence to support that view. I shall draw heavily here on David E. Apter and Tony Saich, *Revolutionary Discourse in Mao's Republic* (Cambridge, Mass., 1994) though many other sources have influenced these comments.

Mao's utopia was in the future not the past. Formally that rules him out of the category of fundamentalist. But does it really? His image of an egalitarian cooperative future is, at least in my judgment, about as far from any prospective reality as any fundamentalist picture of idyllic farm life in pre-industrial America. Mao, of all world leaders, was certainly one of Burkhardt's great simplifiers. Clearly he was anti-intellectual in two senses. He distrusted people who just did mental work as opposed to manual work. He was also highly suspicious of anyone whose ideas might compete with his own. Whether one can consider Mao antirational is a more difficult question to answer. He had an earthy appreciation of technology. There was none of the late twentieth-century antiscientific and antirationalist strain in Mao. Yet his extreme no-nonsense, no-fancy-new-theory way of thinking is an intellectual pattern quite congenial to the fundamentalists left behind and confused by contemporary intellectual trends. A Chinese nationalist under a paper-thin Marxist veneer, Mao was no ordinary hater of things foreign. Here, too, however, his attitude appears to have been extremely instrumental. Foreign things and people were welcome only so long as they would promote his changing conception of the revolution.

As for the use of violence, more and more evidence has been coming out about the large numbers of people who died as a result of Mao's policies as well as about his personal ruthlessness in using the secret police to destroy his enemies. This behavior brings to mind that of God in the Old Testament, certainly a major figure for western fundamentalist movements. Mao was also a "back to basics" figure in Marxism, as nearly all distinguished leaders of the movement have been at some time. Mao had little or no use for the leaders of the USSR, not even Stalin, and for good political reasons. Yet he used Marxism as one justification among others, for his policy of breaking with the first socialist state. One goes back to alleged basic truths, in order to establish a new orthodoxy.

On the basis of this evidence I suggest that there is such a thing as leftist fundamentalism with strong chauvinist overtones, and that Mao presents a good model of it. He is a better model than Lenin because he did succeed in mobilizing masses of Chinese for the sake of revolution. If he had died in 1949 at the moment of revolutionary success, he would have joined the pantheon of the great liberators of mankind. As a matters now stand, leftist fundamentalism is very much out of fashion. But there are already signs that overtly reactionary fundamentalists are casting about for popular grievances on which they can ride to power. Conceivably the ghost of Mao, properly recostumed to suit the occasion, could again become a force with which to reckon.

From the standpoint of estimating the main contours of human affairs a generation and more from now, there is precious little to be gained in seeking more detail about fundamentalism and its prospects. Though vulnerability to this political plague is greater in the poorer parts of the globe, the prosperous West is far from immune. Viewed from a distance the politics of the end of the twentieth century begins to look like a sea of smoldering ashes, known as institutions, with scatterings of sparks from fundamentalist movements. No doubt that is a gross exaggeration, though hardly more so than the packaged optimism of some second tier western politicians.

Fundamentalism, after all, is only one trend among many, even if it is the most ominous. In taking one last look at the bequests of our century to the next it is appropriate to mention again the encouraging ones. As C. Vann Woodward remarked, the inevitable needs all the opposition it can get because it is generally unpleasant. There are good reasons for holding that some major scourges of the twentieth century, Stalinism, Fascism, concentration camps, and world wars may sharply diminish. Unemployment poses a much bigger question mark, especially for nonwestern countries. Even for them it is impossible to rule out the prospect that the horrors of poverty and disease may, in say another half century, be brought under control by methods that are not altogether repressive. All this, one has to grant without the usual bromide that it can happen only if there are enough men of good will.

The reason for rejecting that condition is simple. Along with the rise of antirationalism, the decline in the influence of good will is the most obvious of the threatening trends in the last years of our century. Good will refers to rough and ready rules found in many cultures. Fairly often religion endorses them, though usually only for persons of the same religion. By and large its essence, for the purposes at hand, is to give the other person or group a leg up or "a break" when there is real trouble, and to treat other people as human beings so far as possible within the constraints of a social relationship and without concern for the color of their skin. How widely these ever applied in the past and the extent to which they can be applied in the present are legitimate and very important questions beyond any discussion here. It may also be a bit unfair to assert that the decline of good will is obvious when there are so many books about cultural decline, the end of community, the rise of mass society, and the like. The trouble is that the diagnoses and remedies in these works — to restore or establish community, religion, free enterprise, bigger and more loveable capitalism, neo-socialism, fundamentalism with a human face and so on — are so dubious that they are difficult to take seriously.

This writer has no special diagnosis and remedy for the decline of good will and other maladies. But one last comment, very much in the spirit of William Graham Sumner, must therefore serve to bring closure. The generalization about human affairs that has probably the most empirical evidence behind it holds that human beings find it extraordinarily difficult to work together peacefully for shared and humane purposes. Yet somehow they manage now and then to do so, if often under duress and despite their inclinations.

Index

Age of Discoveries, 3
Agrarian societies, class system, 130–131
AIDS, 109, 172–173
Alexander III, 62
American Revolution, 84, 87
Anti-social behavior
    definitions, 2, 101, 113
    environment and, 103
    fraud and, 105–106
    industry and, 102
    modern civilization and, 114–115
    movements and, 117–118
    political disintegration, 104–105
    remedies for, 116–118
    rights and, 101–102, 117
    social obligations and, 102–103
Appleby, R. Scott, 174
Apprenticeship, 10–11, 12
Apter, David E., 175
Aristocracy. See also under Moral codes
    shift to merchant class, 2–4, 25–26
    wager of law and, 5–6
Aristotle, 146
Arkwright, Richard, 19–22, 30–31, 43
Art, emotional reactions and, 164
Asceticism, 28, 55
Ashton, T. S., 19, 33, 42
Aśoka, 63
Assize, 4
Athens, 133, 145–148
    male autonomy in, 149–150
Austerity, 56. See also Asceticism;
    Carthusians

Authority
    abuse of, 137–138
    capitalism and, 51–52
    communal movements and, 65–66, 68–
        70, 79
    domestic peace and, 136
    economy and, 136–137
    equality and, 115
    justice and, 136
    kibbutz movement and, 68–70
    market and, 60–61, 142
    medieval moral personality and, 15
    obedience to, 10, 15
    oppression and, 136–141
    self-aggrandizement and, 137
    social obligations to, 103–104

Bacon, Francis, 17
Bankers, 26
Bankruptcy, 27
Barclay, John, 65
Barkai, Haim, 69
Behaviorism, 116–117
"Bequests of the Nineteenth Century
    to the Twentieth" (Sumner), 168–
    169
Black markets, 106–107
Bona fide possession, 8
Boulton, Matthew, 20, 22, 34
Bourgeoisie, 94–95
Bruno, St., 78
Buchanan, A., 38
Buddhism, 55, 57–58, 63–64, 77

The Wilder House Series in Politics, History and Culture

CPSIA information can be obtained
at www.ICGtesting.com
Printed in the USA
LVHW020325271118
598297LV00004B/458/P

9 781501 726415